Split-Open Planet

Split-Open Planet

Jidi Majia

REGENT PRESS
Berkeley, California
2021

Copyright © 2021 by Jidi Majia

[paperback]
ISBN 13: 978-1-58790-579-7
ISBN 10: 1-58790-579-5

[e-book]
ISBN 13: 978-1-58790-580-3
ISBN 10: 1-58790-580-9

Library of Congress Catalog Number: 2021036831

Drawings by Jidi Majia

PREFACES
by
Jack Hirschman
Tomas Venclova
Adonis

REGENT PRESS
Berkeley, California
www.regentpress.net

BRIEF BIOGRAPHY of Jidi Majia

A Yi Chinese, one of the most representative poets in contemporary Chinese literature, Jidi Majia's literary career has spanned over thirty-five years and has won international acclaim by having 90 collections of poetry and prose translated into 40-odd languages. He at present serves in the capacity of vice-chairman of China Writers Association.

Major works include: *The Song of My First Love; Self-portrait and Other Poems; The Dream of a Yi Native; The Eagle's Wing and the Sun; Fire and Words; I, the Leopard…; From the Leopard to Mayakovsky; 24 Sonnets Dedicated to My Mother; A Great River.*

Major literary honors conferred: Top prize for the 3rd Edition of New Poetry Contest; Guo Moro Literary Prize; Zhuang Zhongwen Literature Prize; Sholokhov Memorial Medal for literature; Rougang Literature Prize; Mkhiva Humanitarian Award; Gold Award for Master Soul of Chinese Poetry of International Chinese Poets PEN; Homer European Medal of Poetry and Art; Excellent Poetry Prize for Romania Contemporanal Magazine; Bucharest City Poetry Prize; Silver Willow Lifetime Achievement Award at Xu Zhimo Poetry Festival, King's College Cambridge; the Janicki Literary Prize; the Tadeusza Micińskiego Prize; the Medal of Zygmunta Krasińskiego; the Guayaquil International Poetry Prize.

Jidi Majia has initiated a number of high-profile international poetic events such as Qinghai Lake International Poetry Festival, Qinghai International Poets Tent Roundtable Forum, Liangshan & Qinghai International Poetry Week, Chengdu International Poetry Week, etc.

Translated by Huang Shaozheng

PREFACE

Jack Hirschman

In my introduction to the poetry and addresses of Jidi Majia in the 2017 book of his work, *From the Snow Leopard to Mayakovsky,* published by Kallatumba Press, the press of the Revolutionary Poets Brigade of San Francisco, I made the strong point that I believe that in the name of the meaning of international peace Jidi Majia is deserving of nothing less than the Nobel Prize for Literature.

Not only has that thought deepened in me over the past four years, but now with his new book of poems and lectural texts, *Split Open Planet,* published here by the very internationally engaging Regent Press of Berkeley, it is increasingly amazing to me that this great poet has still not received that highest of literary awards. What is astounding about this book is how much one learns about life through the feelings evoked by Jidi Majia's poems, addresses and even two interviews of his development and humane affirmations.

Indeed, one learns so much, from his opening poems about the people and poets of Bucharest and Romania—fascinating in itself because in fact Romania as subject matter of poems is very rare, even exotic. Indeed, one of its greatest poets, Nichita Stanescu, is barely known in the Western, let alone the Chinese, world.

And Jidi Majia's poem to Simon Ortiz, the Acoma Native American poet, certainly has called out his own Nuoso Yi people's ethnic identity and empathy, for that "tribal" dimension in China is not only welcomed but strongly affirmed, contrary to the anti-Chinese propaganda. The Yi people, into which Jidi Majia was born, are a mountain people centered near both Vietnam and Tibet, and he himself is the Vice-Director of the Chinese Writers' Association.

He is also a member of the World Poetry Movement, centered in Medellin, Colombia, as I am, and his address in praise of Fernando Rendon, the head of the WPM as well as of the extraordinary International Poetry Festival in that city, is notable, as is the extraordinary title poem, Split Open Planet, a 10-page tour de force.

This Preface is followed by two more, including a marvelous poem to Jidi Majia by Adonis. I'll close this Preface with an Arcane of my own to Jidi Majia, with best wishes to the reader as he experiences the marvelous poems and other texts of this great Chinese poet.

1

You and I were fated
to be comrades for life,
Jidi Majia.

Even before we met
for your 5th Qinghai Lake
International

Poetry Festival
in Xining and you visited
Aggie's and my room

with Jami Proctor-Xu
and bottles of baijiu. In fact
30 years ago

when you were a young
man and I was
translating Albanian

poetry and found
I loved best of all the words
Xhuxhimaxhuxha,

I realize now
I was rhythmically destined
to meet you as

not only the Chairman
of the All China Writers
Union, but the major

poet of one of
the 56 minorities
in China, the Yi

people, — you, of
the Nuosu "black" strain in
that tribe, no doubt why

you could pen such a
magnificent ode to Nelson
Mandela and

receive the torrential
applause of the Yellow,
Yangtze, and Lancang

Rivers that Qinghai is the
birthplace of, under fireworks
of bursting buckwheat,

as we spoke of how
I was a kabbalist Jew,
and you might be one too,

and this said with heart
and humor as Jami
translated us from

me to you and you to me,
we laughing all the way to
the bottoms of our glasses.

2

And so you had me sit
next to you at all the meals,
the American communist,

and I toasted, toasted
with one Chinese poet or
prefecture after another,

and we toasted each other
with those tiny, delicate jiggers
of Moutai baijiu

and that slowly spinning
table flooded with dishes
of all tasty sorts,

and the next day bussed
to Qinghai Lake and there
— if I'd not already

sensed it — we realized
what a great international
revolutionary you are

by seeing the wall that's
even Greater than the Great Wall,
the Wall of poets

with images of Pablo Neruda,
Langston Hughes, Cesar Vallejo,
Nelly Sachs,

Walt Whitman, Du Fu,
Mahmoud Darwish, Guo
Muruo, William Blake

Yongyuan, richu,
riluo, xiantian qiutian
dongtian chuntian!

Forever, sunrise
sunset, summer autumn
winter spring!

And rectangularly
from the Wall out over a
field of grass, 24

hugh statues of figures
in the epic poems of the world,
from Gilgamesh, to the Song

of Roland, to Beowulf,
to the Kalevala of Finland,
and the epic of Armenia

in what is without doubt
the greatest homage to the art
of poetry in the world.

3

My chubby brilliant
friend, you who said, "Robots
don't bloom", and that

poetry "has become
an affirmation of the
deeply held human

longing to return
to where we came from…to our
spiritual Garden of Eden"

certainly with poems
and brilliant essays, Festivals
and other projects

have done enough to
earn a Nobel Prize for the
nobility of poetry

as the innate language
of the people of the earth
in its song of raising

the banner of human
Kindness and Beauty over
all and every one

of the more than thirty
countries that China graced with
unforgettable welcome,

with avalanches
of books, red cashmere scarves
and the colorful

costumes of the Yi
into whose minority
of eight million

souls we all were
admitted as honorary
members for life.

Bravo! I shout, who
taught you that word
that now, at the end

of every performance,
you shout out, Bravo!
with glee galore;

and, as always with China,
there wants to be, unendingly,
more. More. MORE!

Jack Hirschman was born in New York City in 1933. He has published more than a hundred books of poetry, half of them translations from nine languages. His major work is *The Arcanes*, published in 2006, the year he was elected as the Poet Laureate of the City of San Francisco, till 2009. He is a founding member of the Revolutionary Poets Brigade (RPB) in San Francisco in 2009 (there are now 10 Brigades, 5 in the U. S. and 5 in Europe), and a founding member of the World Poetry Movement (WPM) in Medellin, Colombia in 2011. He was invited to attend Medellin International Poetry Festival, Qinghai Lake International Poetry Festival.

JIDI MAJIA: AN OUTSTANDING PRODUCT OF WORLD MULTICULTURALISM

Tomas Venclova

For hundreds and thousands of years, Chinese literature has developed in its own unique way, almost wholly isolated from Western tradition. The reasons for this include geographical isolation (of which the Great Wall is an emblem), a unique social structure and, perhaps most importantly, the unique features of its ideographic writing system. Viewed from another perspective, Chinese culture has exerted an often-decisive influence on other Far-Eastern cultures. Among the remarkable fruits that emerged from Chinese ancient literary canon was classical lyrical poetry. Chinese people take pride in such poets as Qu Yuan, Tao Yuanming, Li Bai and Du Fu, all of whom belong in the front rank of world poets such as Homer, Horace and Petrarch. Yet prior to the 18th century, classical Chinese literature was virtually unknown in the Western world.

In the 19th and especially in the 20th centuries, the Far East underwent large-scale opening to the West. People in America and Europe took a strong interest in the Far East, and the reverse was also true. Poetry from the Far East began influencing the world's modern literature. At the same time, currents from Europe, America, Russia and even Poland permeated Chinese culture, although this was sometimes delayed. What interfered with this process, aside from huge disparities between cultures, was the complex and difficult road of development which China traveled and continues to travel. Today we are still weathering the turbulent currents of interpenetration between East and West. We can find proof of this fact in Jidi Majia's creative works. He is one of the foremost Chinese contemporary poets, and he is one of the most renowned cultural figures in China today.

As a poet, Jidi Majia stands out from the crowd, even though his poems were forged by the widespread cultural currents of our new world era. He writes in Chinese, but he belongs to the eight-million-strong Yi ethnic group, otherwise known as the Nuosu, who live in mountain areas not far from Vietnam and Thailand. Thus we can say that there is an additional layer of distance between this poet and our culture. Even so, European readers can readily understand his poems.

The Yi People speak a language which belongs to the Tibeto-Burmese language family, and they have an independently developed writing system. Their culture preserves archaic elements related to animistic beliefs. Even now the Yi People put their trust in shamans (which they call Bimos). Bimos preside over weddings, cremations and ceremonies of childbirth. They make offerings to deities of mountains, trees, boulders and the four elements of earth, air, fire and water. The Yi language and writing system is now being taught in schools, but this has not always been the case.

Jidi Majia's mentor was China's eminent poet Ai Qing. In his youth Jidi Majia pored over works of China's classical and twentieth-century literature, as well as Western literature. Yet his heart has remained tied to his own ethnic group—to that primal world view handed down by the Yi Minority which, being unknown to the world's major populations, holds an appealing novelty. Jidi Majia earnestly sympathizes with every ethnic group whose fate is beset by difficulties. His poems are extremely expressive, free-wheeling and rich in metaphor. In his frequently hyperbolic language and his "roots-seeking" orientation, he has an affinity with post-modernist currents. Jidi Majia is strongly attached to use of folkloric elements, in a way that approaches magical realism. His writings are informed by the poetic practice of Africa, Europe and America. Readers will readily notice a strong stylistic connection to Pablo

Neruda, Octavio Paz and poets of the "Negritude" school. In his works we can also trace a literary connection with eastern European poets, from Czeslaw Milosz to Desanka Maksimović. He links up these Western sources with Chinese and Far Eastern tradition, especially with ageless myths and legends from the Yi People, to achieve wondrous and unexpected effects.

For readers who endeavor to understand the era we live in, Jidi Majia's poems offer food for thought which will surely strike a chord of shared feeling.

Translated by Denis Mair

Tomas Venclova (1937-) is a Lithuanian poet, scholar and translator. He is a professor of Slavic Languages and Literature at Yale University and has been grouped with Czeslaw Milosz and Joseph Brodsky as one of the three "Masters from Eastern Europe". He is recognized as one of Europe's greatest poets.

الوقت يكسرُ عقاربَ ساعاته *
تحيّة إلى جيدي ماجيا وشعره

أبجديةٌ حزنٍ: جسدُ العالم، اليومَ،- وقتٌ
يَكسرُ الوقتُ فيه عقاربَ ساعاتِه،
ويقول لأيّامه:
ألعبُ النردَ مع نجمة
أتنبّأـ هل سيكون الدواءُ خميرةَ داءٍ؟
وماذا يقول بريدُ الفضاء
آتيا ذاهبا في حرير الهواء؟

أ تراني ألقي حجابا على كلّ شيء؟ ولكن
هل سأحجب وجهي
بمنديل حبٍّ
أم بمنديل ربٍّ؟
وأنا، لا طريقي طريقي، ولا خطاي خطايا
هل أسائل وجهًا،
أم أسائل مرآتِه؟
ما أقلَّ الوجوهَ وما أكثرَ المرايا.

أتُراها الحياةُ هنا وهناك، شرقا وغرباً،
متاهاتُ ظنٍّ؟
أتراها الفراديسُ تُغلق أبوابَها؟

الجذورُ، جراحُ الجذور نداءٌ وشوقٌ
للتمرُّد في كَنَف الأبجديّة،
ضدَّ ما سُمِّي الأبديّة.

بين ميْتٍ وميْتْ
ميِّتْ آخرـ لماذا

* *Translation follows on page xxi.*

نسي القاتلون اسمَه؟

لا فواصلَ، لا حركات
في الكتاب الذي كتبتُه تباريحُ أعمالنا وأيّامنا:
كلماتٌ
تتناسلُ في كلمات
تتناثرُ في مَهْمَهٍ.

شغفي يقرأ الآن ما يتيسّرُ: جرحٌ
نازفٌ كوكبيٌّ
خدعتْهُ نبوءاتُه.

الرمادُ احتفاءٌ بأنقاضه:
الرمادُ،
وفيٌّ لمواعيده.

أتُراها القصيدةُ تقدر أن تحضنَ الوُجودَ وأن تتهجَّى
من جديد تقاطيعَه وتجاعيدَه؟
هي ذي وردةُ الشعر تبكي أصدقاءَ طفولاتِها- تغنّي:
لن أقاتلَ إلا بعِطري.

كيف يحدثُ أن تصبح الأرضُ صوتا
لا يقول سوى موتِها؟
كيف يحدث أن تصبح السماءُ دمًا سائلا
على كلّ وجهٍ؟

أدونيس
باريس، أواخر أكتوبر، 2020

أدونيس، ولد عام 1930 في سورية. شاعر ومفكر وناقد أدبي كبير ذاع صيته في العالم العربي، ويعتبر أحد أهم الشعراء في عالمنا اليوم. يرى كثير من النقاد أن تأثيره في الشعر العربي المعاصر يشبه تأثير عزرا باوند وإليوت في اشعار اللغة الإنجليزية.

Time is Pulverizing the Clock Hands
—In Honor of Jidi Majia and his poems

1
Grief-laden letters, this body of today's world,
within which time is pulverizing the clock hands
and telling the days:
"I'm throwing dice with a star
I predict: will medicine become the cause of illness?
The postman in space is draped in silk air
shuttling back and forth; what is he transmitting?"

2
Am I putting on a veil for all living things? But,
am I covering my face
with love's scarf
or god's scarf?
The road really isn't my road, these steps really aren't my steps
Should I ask a face,
or ask a mirror?
How few faces are, how plentiful mirrors are!

3
In this place or that, East or West,
has life already become a subjective maze?
Has heaven already closed its gates?

4
The roots, the roots' wounds, are in the bosom of letters
shouting out and looking forward
to all so-called "eternal" rebellions

5
Between the dead and the dead
more people are dying; why
have their murderers forgotten their names?

6
The pain of our daily labor, the books we write
have no punctuation marks, have no syllables
Words multiply within words
and drift in barrenness

7
Now, I ride with lax reins,
 flip through books
There are wounds wherever my eyes reach:
the planet is bleeding, deceived by the oracle

8
Ashes are congratulating ruins
Ashes
are faithful to their own promises

9
Can poems embrace existence;
can they once again describe the face and wrinkles of existence?
The roses of poems are crying for childhood friends, chanting:
We only rely on fragrance to fight

10
How has the earth become one voice
that only knows how to speak of its own death?
How has the sky become one bloodstain
that flows on every face?

—Adonis
October, 2020, Paris
Translated by Jami Proctor Xu
(Translated from the Chinese translation of the Arabic.)

Adonis (1930-) is the most significant poet, ideologist, literary theorist in the Arab world. He is honoured as a great master in the world of poetry today. Critics say that Adonis has had a profound influence on modern Arabic poertry..

Catalog

POEMS

3	Double Meaning
4	For My Statue in Herculane —For Ilya Cristescu
5	At the Gravesite of Nichita Stanescu
6	Grand Canal
7	I Will Always Feel Love for Meek Lives
9	The Power of a Mouth Harp
10	Praise Song for a Saddle
15	Birth and Death of an Eagle
21	The Flaw in Human Nature
23	Someone Whose Name I Can't Say
25	To Our Way of Thinking…
26	A Flyting Spoken to Oneself
27	For Nicanor Parra
29	A Soldier and a Stone from Diaoyu Fortress
31	Shang Mound, There Is No Ending
32	Yet My Song Is Offered to Fleeting Lives
33	As for Us…
34	The Secret Language of Poems…
35	A Poet in His Waning Years
36	For My Father's Generation
37	My Sister's Woolen Cape
38	Jaw Harp Master —For Edi Rihuo
39	Indian —For Simon Ortiz
41	The Ruins of Nizi Malie
42	Once I Saw…
43	Poet
45	Jewish Graveyards
46	José María Arguedas
48	Juan Gelman
49	An Alternate Explanation of Freedom
50	Great River —To the Yellow River
57	Disputation Over the Flames
64	Who is Faster, Us or Death —To all who beat against COVID-19 in 2020

71	Split Open Planet — For all of humankind and all living things
92	Late Elegy — For my father, Jidi Zuozhuo Wuhelüeqie
104	Another Springtime
105	Ladle
106	Carriage Outside of Time
107	Stone
108	Firepit of the Earth
109	Give Back to the World
111	The Mountains of Yesterday, Today, and Tomorrow
114	Zizipuwu

Drawings

117

Literary lectures and interviews

137   Du Fu's Thatched Cottage—Both A Reality and A Legend
— *Address at the Opening Ceremony of 2017 International Festival of Poetry & Liquor*

140   A City Hemmed in with Radiant Beams of Poetry
— *Address at the Opening Ceremony of 2017 Chengdu International Poetry Week*

146   Heavenly Stones Made of Eagle Wings and Light
— *Remarks at the Opening Ceremony of the 2nd Liangshan, Xichang Silk Road Intl Poetry Week*

150   Poets Are Still the Moral Leaders of the Civic Society Today
— *Written replies to Graham Mort*

158   To Create Differently: From Juan Rulfo to Octavio Paz
— *A speech given at a seminar held in Peking University marking the 45th anniversary of Sino-Mexico diplomatic relations*

168   Word as Salt ·an Alternative Human Paradise Made of Light
—Transparence and Dimness of Poetic Diction
— *Address at the Opening Ceremony of 2018 Zigong "Belt and Road" International Poetry Week*

173   Narcissistic Self —Seeking Is Not the Sole Responsibility of a Decent Poet
— *Acceptance Speech at the Awarding Ceremony of Tadeusza Micińskiego Prize*

176   Poets Empowered by a Mysterious, Dark and Burning Sound
— *Address at 2019 4th Xichang Qinghai Silk Road International Poetry Week*

180   Forces Hidden in Poetry: Let's Make a Rendezvous with Tradition!
— *Address at the 6th Qinghai Lake International Poetry Festival*

185	Poetry, a Tribute to Love, an Arsenal Against All Violence — *A keynote address delivered at the Sino-Czech Roundtable on Literature on the Commemoration of the 70th Anniversary of Sino-Czech Republic Cultural Exchange and the Independent Czechoslovak State Day*
191	The Meaning, Dissemination and Inner Secrecy of Poetry — *Address at the seminar of 3rd International Poetry & Liquor Conference*
194	Let Poetry Empower Us Strongly for Marching Toward Tomorrow and Future — *An Address on 2020 Kritya Poetry Festival, India*
197	The Sun Will Still Rise Tomorrow — *Speech for the Opening Ceremony of the Thirtieth Medellin International Poetry Festival*
200	Paying Tribute to the Rivers, Mountains, and Oceans — *Acceptance speech for the 2020 Guayaquil International Poetry Award*
203	A Sheep, a Farmer and a Poet's Steady Gaze — *Presentation of the 2020 "1573 International Poetry Prize" and Preface of Lucina Schynning in Silence of the Nicht: A Selection of Poems by Eiléan Ní Chuilleanáin*
206	Let Poetry be the Path Leading to Each Heart: Answers to the Questions from the Organizing Committee of 14th World Poetry Festival of Venezuela
214	A Round of Applause for a World that is Diverse, Rich, Always Different and Symbiotic — *Address to the 14th Venezuelan World Poetry Festival*
217	Weeping for Der Zor — *A Preface to Sona Van's A LIBRETTO FOR THE DESERT and the Laudation for 573 International Poetry Prize of 2019*

Poems

Double Meaning

On his deathbed, the poet Nichita Stanescu[1]
Said to the doctor who tried to save him,
"Please give me some of your youth!"
This was said in a spirit of praise and yearning
    for life,
Showing appreciation for bygone days he'd lived through.
As a fleshly reality, a horse will pass into nothingness:
Whether that time comes in the night, or in long hours
Of sunlight…the day will come when a nail no longer affixes
A skull and its slumber to the vault of sky.
Perhaps it will not be a lingering glance,
But only death in the most conventional form.
If we say that the existence of a thinking entity
Is itself a nothingness, yet by no means imaginary,
Then no wonder, for one who leads a human life,
To play hide-and-seek with other shadows
Is sufficient to exhaust a spiraling lifetime.
Though life's magnetic field is in no way bland and dull,
This proves to be a double meaning, imputed to it by the living.
Perhaps for this reason, only life's absurd engagements
Along with abstracted words, guided by light,
Can repeatedly meet darkness and death with refusal.

[1] Nichita Stanescu (1933-1983) was a famous Romanian poet and representative figure of modernist literature.

Translated by Denis Mair

For My Statue in Herculane[1]
—*For Ilya Cristescu*[2]

Oh, Ilya Cristescu,
My eyes
Are in Herculane.
My eyes, calling up visions
Of a quiet ocean, transparent spheres
Hills and rivers, cities and shrines…
My eyes, in the name of ten-thousand things,
Open the stage curtain of darkness and light;
Perhaps this is the unity of center and margin.
My eyes, if they are brimming with tears,
This must be…and can only be the sorrow
Of Herculane, making me weep in spite of myself.
My eyes show the hint of a smile
Because the one-and-only Herculane
Was praised at a banquet by poems in many languages.
My ears
Are in Herculane
Like the soliloquy of an insect that subsides
Into the white interior of thought;
My ears know the black hole of a stone's totality;
They hear the outcry of crushed rock, the womb of silence,
Like a star plunging from above, an iron band to crown one's head,
But only my mouth still waits, in Herculane
For the day I will enter its body
And serve as the voice for its heart.

[1] Herculane is a walled town in eastern Romania.
[2] Ilya Cristescu is a well-known Romanian poet and a professor at Romania Western University.

Translated by Denis Mair

At the Gravesite of Nichita Stanescu

Had it been one minute later
The gate of this cemetery where your body rests
Would have been closed under encroaching darkness.
Due to your sleeping posture under the mud
The axe of time has become your shield.
By this time, your arm is a flute of bone;
Words will become the piping of another shadow,
Staring eyes will pass through the stone of darkness,
Thought's gaze climbs vine-like around eternity's backbone,
A passing guest swallows up the steel rails of language;
He gulps down famished stars and the pillar of nothingness.
When life turns into a darkened carriage
When death defines your contour
And your unyielding skull overlooks the stars,
Only your truthful poems, like a great bird,
Will drift quietly through the sky over Romania.

Translated by Denis Mair

Grand Canal

Not all alterations wrought by mankind
Upon nature are acts of destruction
Though some have lasted thousands of years.
A great and multi-faceted example of this
Is the excavation of the Grand Canal…
When clinking metal opened the earth's body
And winged masts swelled with lungfuls of freedom
History was rewritten in wavery images on water,
Heavenly bodies revolved above a hastening boat;
Its oars sounded pleasantly along with a split stone bell.
A durable sluice was dug, until a mass of raw iron settled
Upon a route. Words were fixed in lofty positions of stars,
Not by height of mountains or strength of wind…
Pristine water is what made this miracle:
Scepter of rulers. Pillars for palaces. Grain-ears for war.
Life-pulse of empire. Tipped-over goblet. Mobile treasury.
Wealth nurtured by water. Threat dispelled by salt.
Blood transfused to power's center. Secret files of political foes.
Diffusing dialects. Women's sobs. Genuineness or contrivance.
Transacted appeasements. Riverbed that buried conspiracies.
Relative existence of nothingness. Death that goes on living.

How unlucky, if the Grand Canal has no more water
All the freight it carried will become fragmentary memories
And stars showing intermittently through clouds.

Translated by Denis Mair

I Will Always Feel Love for Meek Lives

I always feel love for the meekest lives,
Perhaps my partiality toward them is inborn.

In our world, powerful things are imposing enough
Laying claim to rotations of stars in the name of truth and justice
Holding the sword of solar radiance to defend morality's rules,
Yet ancient barbaric crimes are still happening
In Libya and Afghanistan, in today's Jerusalem,
From the resistance of Kosovo to blood feuds of Chechnya
In bleeding Iraq and weeping Syria.

Also in Somalia, still mired in civil war today,
And the sites of criminality are not just in these places
Numbers of slaughtered innocents are still increasing.
Admittedly the salvation of souls has not stopped for a day
But when confronted by screams and moans of the blameless
We are unable to save them from the hell of the human realm.

I do not know the true distance between heaven and earth
But I can distinguish the demonic from the angelic.
Oh! Whose hand is this hurling dice into the air?
Why does the meek side so often suffer punishment?

I always feel love for the meekest lives;
Perhaps my partiality for them is inborn.
Those meek lives are right next to us
Distributed in every corner of the world,
In dark shade, like a congealed teardrop
Or a broken-voiced folksong in the mother tongue,
These sounds overlooked by so-called powerful people

Are remote, backward, weak. They are never
At the center defined by the dominant civilization. Yet I
Have chosen to stand by their side.

Translated by Denis Mair

The Power of a Mouth Harp

Sound as fine as floss
From depths of the good earth and the cosmos,
A cry that penetrates
Right into the blood:
My heart
Has begun
Beating outside the body
Like a stalwart
Of our tradition
Still on the battle line;
Such was my merit
Won in battle:
With a mouth harp
I once warded off
The attack of an orchestra.

Translated by Denis Mair

Praise Song for a Saddle

During silence, the wheel of time does not stop.

One: **Waiting**

Recalling the gold of past times
Only the horseman is awake;

Wind blows past the eyeball;

It blows past a skull's black stare,
A bellied-out cape, gesturing motions
Of freedom that merge into an aura…

Son of the eagle
Invisible other half of wings
Manifested in entities of light…

Soaring inwardly through
What is unresolved, secret of origin
Extinguished on a bird's wing…

Honor exalted
Above life…a halo of death
Shimmers in the lap of ranged mountains;
A horseman still sleeps in a verse of praise
But the flute-notes of dawn
Defended by flames
Have begun their advance.

Two: **The Implicit Sense of a Symbol**

The horseman has no name,
His names line up as rungs on a ladder.

The saddle's seat only recalls victors,
Only a receding shape, a backlit posture
Forever heading forward, melting into darkness.

Hollowness behind eyes suffused with light,
Fingers of wind tightly clasp at the back…
The horse's backbone is a straight line;
Movement and stillness die in relation to each other;
Revolving mountains fall into the blue;
Sky-vault and broad land slip away from time.

Ears incline toward the blankness of existence
Which enters extinction in a flitting instant.
Eye of needle. Black hole. Infinity. Blind spot.
A sound pervades and reaches of the cosmos
In cyclic succession, without a goal…
Incantations congeal in the throat, then fade away.

Oh horseman, whatever your bloodline
Be it violet or black or white
Contention on horseback favors the valiant.
He has no crevice, refuses to draw a shameful breath;
Undying honor is more noble than life.
Look, what a great speed, passing through a ribcage!
Only on such scales can the high and low be distinguished.

Three: **Shadow of a shod hoof**

Forever unflagging…
At every curve, its absolute balance
Bids farewell to nothingness.
Contours of limbs undulate freely
Treading the land's flowers in full bloom;
An overlapping flight of countless phantoms,
A forward-tilting body stabbing into the future,
Nothing above its shoulders but swaying tips.

Its galloping limbs are suspended in mid-air,
Seeds are strewn, that were fertilized
At the core of an invisible womb.
On the far side of that continuance
There is no burning arrow.
Praises of the steed named Daliyazong
Have been handed down in the iris of words,
Not stretched in blank spaces of consciousness,
Yet it witnesses a horseshoe plunging downward.
For stalwarts whose valor is undying, there is no need
To prove where remains are buried on native ground;
You need only gaze with lowered head to find
A leaf-like flake of fragmentary iron.

Four: **The Three-Color Primordium**

Weight of blackness goes straight to the marrow:
That is the secret of late evening's fluidity,
Color of the broad land's heart,
A scepter's comings and goings, firmly upright…

In the meditative silence of a soul,
There is none of that, or I should say, its nobility
Is forever above that of gold
Watched over by near celestial bodies…

Earrings of the sun,
Cogitation with an influx of light,
Oh, eternal metal,
Massive cup brimming.

Grab the hair of the ten-thousand things,
Blow air out of a bared chest
Liable to flee from another celestial vault
With its tongue-tip of words that licked iron.

Crimson coloration of flowing blood

From the ox or sheep offered for slaughter,
Red vessel of life
Water thirsting for stone.

Only by blood that contains salt
Admixed with the frenzy of minerals
Can that hand reach out for
The fruit of a ripe breast.

It has opened out to us,
The most powerful part of electricity,
Having no other colors
Only red and yellow and black;
From before birth and after death
They are memory in the purest form.

Five: **Silent Stage Prop**

One can hear the soundless neigh
But the horse cannot be seen;
Flames pass through rock walls and star clusters.
Who calls out the horseman's name?
If not for him, those raised front hooves
Wouldn't smash the existence of nothingness.

That hand grasps the reins
Like a bow's arc on the horse's back
Waiting for the moment to gallop into darkness:
Is it a skeleton's thirst for wind…
Or is it a saddle's wish to be free
That causes the phantom horseman to call
Under moonlight, to that invisible steed?

Blocs of the three-color primordium
Manifest a tranquil light,
Those underlying colors of origin holding
The secret of what was split apart.

Oh, the great charge forward belongs to you alone
Who refuses to enter eternity's slumber.

The time will come, that certain moment
Will descend into the heart of words,
You will suddenly awaken
To soar under the vertical sky,
Without head, without eyes, not even
A tail that streams on the wind.
Your four hooves have been divided into shadows;
Though parted from their fleshly frame
The echo of clopping horseshoes
Still reverberates where sky meets earth.
Indeed, you have brought tidings of victory;
You have notified us ahead of time.

Translated by Denis Mair

Birth and Death of an Eagle

Your birth and death are equal in greatness.

One: **Signs of Hatching in Progress**

Up in the highest place
The only domain
Where a cliff greets daybreak
There is nothing to be seen
Only an egg, unable to spin,
Gate of countless needles' eyes.
There is no "formerly"; all is a beginning,
Air and memory are suspended,
Forgotten before the next incarnation.

A smooth-rubbed stone,
Core of mild, soft water,
This placental chaos;
Another ocean lies therein;
Time churns its yearning waters,
Until those four limbs take shape,
The fist of a beating heart,
Future chest swelling with devotion.

Oh, yes, that is your cosmos; outside of it,
Is the macrocosm; down from the sky-vault
Sifts light of gosling yellow,
With no meaning the mouth can utter.
A colorless, odorless waterfall can be perceived,
Albeit with no sound, from above to below
It pervades the periphery of thought.

Your breath is not internal;
It is in fibers suffused with sunlight;

It enters a blue, pulsing vein,
An abstraction of one, or of seven[1]—
None else but they could be your father,
Because the umbilical cord of final generation
Is always gripped by them.

Two: Heart of the Heavens

Hail to the sun
And the boundless force that draws things along.
It was you, with your mouth-corners of metal
In the name of birth and resistance
With a sledge-hammer of light that struck
The crown of an upended anvil.
The moment your celestial body splits,
Light bears witness to your birth.
There is no sign of a storm, but daytime lightning
Flickers faintly at the horizon.

When you had not yet appeared
The ancient tradition of patronymics
Had already prepared a name for your coming…
As you view the oceanic sweep of starry space
The plunging of a meteor is as ephemeral
As the frolicking of stars in a dream.
Perhaps you do not understand
The entire meaning of life's nothingness
But by grace of your emergence
The sky's heart was fitted with wheels and wings.
Only because of you, the sky's height
Could be one among other heights,
Elsewise there'd be no black period to end a sentence,

---

[1] An origin myth of the Nuosu people is presented in *Hnewo Tepyy* (The Book of Origins): The female progenitor of the Nuosu people sits weaving in front of her doorway as she watches an eagle fly overhead. After drops of the sacred eagle's blood fall upon her skirt, she becomes pregnant and gives birth to the culture hero Zhyge Alu. In a variant of this epic, the woman Pumo Hniyy is visited by several eagles of different hues. The difference in numbers of eagles—from one to seven—is not important: what matters is the solar lineage of the sacred eagle/eagles. See the version of *Hnewo Tepyy* translated by Mark Bender and Aku Wuwu, in which several eagles are mentioned. (Mark Bender, "Tribes of Snow" in *Asian Ethnology* Volume 67, Number 1 • 2008, 5-42). The version translated by Qubi Shimei in 1978 mentions only one eagle. (Liangshan yiwenzi liaoxuanyi, Leeteyi [Selected Translation of Liang Mountain Yi-Language Materials, Vol. 1, *Hnewo Tepyy*], Southwest Minzu Institute Printing House, Chengdu, 1978) —Tr.

And tripartite whiteness would be mere whiteness.

Moment by moment, with ten thousand beings maintaining
A hidden dialogue and tie of feeling,
Sitting in a nest of dawn
The limpid mirror that reflects your image
Projecting you and your wispy trains of thought
Has already heard, by way of a third party
The black-hole rhythm of your heartbeat.
For the plains and mountains, perhaps you are
A horse, a velocity, a time-honored folk song
That keeps its freshness, and for the sky
Your existence is greater than a numerical total.

Three: **Reclusive Interval**

Only the greatest height can be
Absolutely solitary; in the face of emptiness
Of ideas, language falls prey to thought.
You have 100 postures to choose from
But only one shows the lordly bearing
That turns in a gyre over particles,
An act of floating over a pause in time;
There is no ahead, no behind, no right or left
No above or below, their existence is gone.

No shadow of weight goes through cyclical changes,
It is only a form of soaring,
Turbulence in a gas, a thin edge streaking through
Inwardness, a gigantic invisible force
Lighter than restful slumber,
Bronze gleam on a wing's feathers
Bearing blood-redness of sunset's lingering rays.
There is no going higher, upward is spherical blankness;
A downward look shows rivers thinner than threads
Emitting white mist which appears like white quartz;
Forests are green color blocs unmixed with other hues.

Aside from the fruits that abide off-planet
Your gaze captures traces of everything.

The sliver of a leaf, an ant traversing the ground,
An insect, a rock receiving an alternate kind of caress,
Image projected in a pupil, magnified a thousand times…

Having viewed slaughter between living things
That is the law of nature—to be lawless;
All beings take part in it,
But human sins are especially heavy.

Around a precipice seldom reached by human traces
Such an enigmatic conscious creature
In its flowing movements of departure and return
Leaving only a breath of nullity.

Four: Watching over a Circle

As if watching over rangeland
Never losing sight of any battlefront,
As an organism it defended freedom
And its right to live.

Though the spine's omphalos
Has been riven by the lance of thought,
Even so the stars and moon of words
Still stand at its shoulder;
The shield bequeathed by ancestors
Confronts the buffetings of each storm.

Bearing up under the megalith of a cosmos,
It sucks on old proverbs, and it transports
A wounded wooden bowl to a place of safety.
By strength of that secret talisman
In will soon glide nonchalantly
Between a devil and an angel.

It will inscribe the language of earth and sky
On the entrails of fruition,
If the self's other half be lost
Death by then had surely drawn near.
Hold firm to one pole of the magnet
Or else topple from loss of too much blood.

From skull to tenacious toes, all are divine branches
Bedecking the celestial canopy of the unknown,
And nameless constellations. The hierophant of a tribe
In a dream foretells your final hour of death.

Five: **Funeral**

Once the hour of death's coming is known
Its speed is more rapid than a curse.
Your eyes are stocked full of black salt;
The cords of ancestors harness your spine.

This is a gift, made in offering
To an enduring future, and it is
An apology and salute to life.
Don't admonish creatures with life's meaning;
What they know may encompass even more.

Oh, the skyward road has revealed
Its route into whiteness
Which leads toward the palace of death.
The Soul-Sending Scripture will be chanted repeatedly.
In these times, the rituals of death
Have surpassed those of birth in grandeur,
All of which comes about by itself.

As one's gaze is directed toward the setting sun
The wind speed thereabouts is changing
The direction of eternity, while in a higher place
Violet clouds are still like glass.

Oh look! It is you heading towards the sun's
    position,
Gaining altitude quickly, streaking like a beam
    of light,
Your feathers emit a whizzing sound, flinging
    pain
Like colorless blood into the parted air.

Still you gain altitude, like an arrow out of
    control,
Exhausting your last strength, straining to
    arrive
At the apex of destruction and nothingness.
Yes, you have reached it—a peal of thunder booms,
Amid a dazzling aura you complete the act
That all your ancestors have completed.
This moment, the vast sky subsides to stillness,
Only a few stray feathers are drifting down.[1]

[1] Unlike vultures, corpses of dead eagles are seldom found in the wilderness. This is a mystery of zoology: when eagles die, they apparently disappear, leaving only a few stray feathers. Why?

Translated by Denis Mair

The Flaw In Human Nature

I was in my ancestral home at Dajyshalo,
The hearth-fire was gradually dying down.

Whose hand had written this work of history?
Distant mountains also seemed to listen intently.

Beginning with James Watt's invention in 1781
They waved the banner of steam power to bring
A huge driving force into a world made new.
In wastelands, on oceans, in places humans had yearned to go
When steam whistles of trains released their white vapor
And ships with unheard-of horsepower ploughed through waves.
When the infant of a century was sounding its first wails,
The Wright brothers' plane allowed the dreams of men
To pass through the whiteness of unimaginable heights.
Oh humanity! How could such an achievement
Not fill our hearts with pride and jubilation?
Velocity of steel reached seldom-visited tribes;
While bringing so-called civilization it also brought syphilis.
In any region where people were defined as barbarians
One could hear the sobs of primitive musical instruments.

Whether in ancient Greece or in our own period
This planet's history has not been simple repetition.
As we gaze into vast reaches of starry space
At times we can forget the misfortunes life has undergone,
But torture and slaughter still happen, every hour of the day.
How brightly Edison's light bulbs shine at Christmas;
So many pairs of eyes fill with expectation of New Year,
But Nazi incinerators used electricity to turn living people,
Along with their fear and despair, into ashes.
In fact, today's reality is much like the vanished past:
Wails of Syrian children coming from shell-scarred ruins

Have not moved the killers to put down their weapons.
In the past century, humankind has also gained possession
Of atomic energy, computers, nanotech, metamaterial, robots,
Genetic engineering, cloning, cloud computing, the internet, digital
    currency
And weapons sufficient to destroy all living things.

As ways of treating life, they are often only methods
To kill foes more quickly and precisely. As for latent evil
It has not yet been altered by the baptism of time.

I was reading in my ancestral home at Dajyshalo,
The hearth-fire was gradually dying down.

Translated by Denis Mair

Someone Whose Name
I Can't Say

Who are "the people"? They are men and women rushing past
On an avenue; no two of them have the same facial features.
They are an old man walking in a plaza, his rheumatic legs trembling,
To walk fifty feet, using a cane, seems as hard as climbing to the sky,
Or a youth with a bounce in his step, walking to his academy.
Of course they may be someone you could meet anywhere
Whom you can't call by name, because you never got acquainted.
Is "the people" an idiomatic usage or an abstract term?
As I see it, without the presence of individuals, we would not have
This word that often appears in our speech and texts.
Perhaps "the people" conveys an expansive view of politics,
So when we speak of the sea, it relates somehow to "the people".
Some say that a droplet isn't a sea, just as the person across from us
Is not the people, but is such logic valid?
You could say if it weren't for grains of sand, how could a vast desert
Ever take shape? Yet some would persist in their conception, saying
Sand is to a desert as the wind's movement is to a shadow in the wind.
As for a drop of water, perhaps we ignore its existence;
Only when drops converge into an ocean do we discover
Their value. As for "the people", I have no deep or lofty understanding.
Often it is someone emerging from a subway exit, tired out
By her hectic life, or one who climbs on a scaffold, working hard
All day; it could be one who checks her watch and hurries to pick up
A kindergartner. Although their worries and dreams vary widely
They have one point in common: they are ordinary people.
They pass through cities and villages, through gladness and sadness;
At times they lose focus, due to survival pressures dogging their foot-
    steps,
But as persons they are drops in an ocean: once they disappear into
    blueness
It is hard to seek their traces amid crashing waves.

That is why I believe in the vibrant life of each conscious being.

Translated by Denis Mair

To Our Way of Thinking…

To our way of thinking, the Motherland is not only sky;
It is more than rivers and forest and the fatherly land,
It is also our language, our words and epics down through time.
To our way of thinking, the Motherland is not just a lexicon
Of terms like "ranged mountains", "sun", "beehive" and "hearth";
It is mother's hands that swaddled us and put on holiday finery;
It lies in a mouth harp's secrets…in the family tree each householder
    can recite.
No wonder my mother said to me, before she left this world:
"I have one last request. Please make sure
To send my remains back to where I was born."
To our way of thinking, the Motherland is more
Than a geographical idea: it calls to mind
A taste, a scent, a voice, something in the soil
That is not present anywhere else.
When wandering sons find themselves in far corners of the world
Just singing a verse in their own tongue, that many may not know
They return to an alternate, unseen land—the one that mothered
    them.

Translated by Denis Mair

A Flyting[1] Spoken to Oneself

When a rock passes through the eye of a needle,
The needle's backbone gives off a sound of light.

The needle's eye have ribs that enfold rocks of words,
Without sound, yet lulling to eternal slumber.

That golden raindrop flung from an eagle's wing—
Is it an egg the sky has been hatching?

No it is emptiness from the celestial vault,
But an egg did foretell the birth of a universe.

[1] A "*kne-re*" (similar to the Scots word "flyting") is a performance of wordplay or verbal dueling heard on festive occasions among the Yi people.

Translated by Denis Mair

For Nicanor Parra[1]

In his lifetime he practiced "anti-poetry".
He opposed poems that ought to be opposed.
He was against their irrelevance to human
    reality,
Against them for being drained of blood,
And thus no more than faceless words,
For being aloof and setting themselves above things,
For presuming that they occupy the heights of spirit,
For lyric flights that are hollow and contrived. Of course…
He opposed the manifestoes they thought up.
He often strolled along the beaches of Chile;
His feet left a string of question marks in the sand;
He protruded a questioning tongue at the sky
So he could tell us about the rain's rusty flavor.
He was always anti-poetry, because
So much of poetry has strayed away from the soul,
Away from sorrow of men with different skin colors.
Such a departure has been going on for a long time.
He is "anti-poetry", because the brain of poetry
Has been lingering at the edge of death;
The breasts of words have no fragrant milk,
Their withered womb cannot receive seeds of life.
His existence was a retort to all inanities,
It even hurled mockery at death's blackness,
And it always responded to life with a jest,
Even jeering as his coffin was moved into place,
And sewing a patch on a brand-new shirt.
Now I see news of his funeral in the papers:
Over his coffin was draped
A gaily-patterned quilt
Sewn by his mother in his childhood.
Not everyone can understand
What the message behind this could be.

[1] Nicanor Parra (1914-1976) was one of Chile's most famous poets and a leader of the "anti-poetry" movement. His influence as a poet was felt in Latin America and worldwide.

In fact, he was saying to us:
"This moment marks the grand beginning
Of another game: this time 'anti-death' ".

Translated by Denis Mair

A Soldier and a Stone from Diaoyu Fortress

The lone fortress was under siege, hemmed in on all sides;
Although attacks were mounted at intervals, making the air ring
With whoops and clangs and drumbeats
Leading to more and more casualties each time, yet
Hopes of breaching the fort grew ever slimmer.

Those days of deadlock dragged on and on;
Both sides grew accustomed to this grim game
Joining life and death in an unresolved knot.

Banners over the fortress were a sign:
The will to fight still ran high in their veins.
Folks say their wellhead was at the fort's highest point—
No fear that their water would be cut off or poisoned.
Food and fuel gave them no cause for worry,
What they had in storage would last for years.

The siege was intensifying day by day;
Plans for a renewed assault were underway...

Fortunes of the Borigin clan were at their height
Having just captured the Kipchak chief near the Caspian Sea,
A crack detachment had taken Dali Kingdom in the Southwest;
Their cavalry had crossed the hills and plains of Central Asia;
News of their blitz of victories reached the Mediterranean.
They were poised to clash with the Mamluk Sultanate of Egypt
In a battle to crown the outcome of their westward push,
But here their attack force could not move forward;
Their plan for decisive victory had hit a quagmire.
Both sides were bone-tired, the fight was in deadlock.

Around this time, during the morning hours,

(Had it been afternoon or dusk, what then?)
Mongke Khan[1] once again climbed a lookout
    tower
To see what the fort's defenders were up to.

At the very same hour, on a catapult platform
A soldier gazing across the wall at the enemy
    line
Saw someone viewing the fort from that tower.
(If that soldier hadn't reacted in a certain way,
and if he hadn't taken the following actions,
would things have turned out quite differently?)

Likewise, in the ensuing minute, if that soldier
Had not loaded the catapult, with his squad's help,
And if they hadn't loosed a stone with perfect aim.
(If that stone had fallen a bit short or a bit far,
Or a bit to one side, what would have happened?)

Was this a random event? Was it purely a fluke?
Not every fluke or random event, just by happening,
Can rewrite the obscure causes of history or fate.

The soldier who noticed a man standing on the tower
Had no way of knowing who that man was; still less
Could he have known that the round stone he used
Would play a huge role in steering the fates of men,
Because news of the Khan's death, sent forth that day,
Caused the Khanate's far-flung chieftains to turn homeward.

In official histories, we only see this record:
"1259— The great warrior Mongke Khan died at Diaoyu Fortress."
The scourge of God was broken there!

Translated by Denis Mair

---

[1] Borigin Mongke (1209-1259), the fourth Khan of Mongolia, was the grandson of Genghis Khan (founder of China's Yuan Dynasty). In 1259 Mongke Khan was fatally injured by a catapult projectile while laying siege to Diaoyu Cheng (Fisherman's Fortress in what is now Hechuan District, Chongqing City.)

Shang Mound, There Is No Ending

"Shang Mound" is a name given this place by others.
It is an omphalos engorged by wind and legends.
Before it was named, the people of Shang were here,
Teeth of bronze defended the skyline from the unknown.
Caravans still traverse it, they have never disappeared,
They are just on the other side of time; they are trekking
Into an alternate present that we call the past;
Life and death are merely two forms of experience.

Only sound can pass through different spaces;
Only light can suffuse solid objects.
Reincarnation is not what calls the tune;
Dying and birth occur in endless alternation,
Visions of eternity give way to destruction.
There is no higher place, the tombs of supreme kings
Are under the feet of holiday climbers;
The tombs have been raided countless times,
Moss has coated the walls of stone.
Due to the lure of imagined riches
No one thought to leave king's bones intact.

There is no higher place, because in lower places
People watched their passing—one king after another
Like comets streaking across the firmament.
This mound may be a higher form of being,
No wonder the living are drawn to climb its height
To watch quiet, sunlit water, returning to its source
Across wheatfields of words, as we gaze afar,
Seeing mottled stone blocks of a weathered city wall
In these barrens that undulate to the edge of vision.
There is no past, present or future...just specks of sails,
Now in now out of view, on the depths of time.

Translated by Denis Mair

Yet My Song Is Offered to Fleeting Lives

Precious sword, eagle-talon goblet, agate earrings—
For such things each man has an inborn liking.
A stallion, a cowrie-studded sash, a white wool cape—
Are known as the manliest accoutrements of heroes.
To shape a new life and cherish honor with no fear of death…
Such is the legacy passed down by every clan.
It seems that all of this was made ready for me,
But I am a poet, what I need even more
Is wind of freedom and words abluted by fire,
Dewdrops at dawn, starry sky of boundless indigo,
Muted notes of cradle songs, a lover's sweet nothings…
Along with those, I should possess musical instruments,
An old recorder, a moon guitar, a three-reed jaw harp.
To recite verses for such a world is my mission.
From time immemorial, death has shadowed the living,
Yet my song is offered to fleeting lives.

Translated by Denis Mair

As for Us…

Poetry…perhaps it is the most ancient art,
It has kept humans company for a long time.
Ah, to be a poet is not a profession, because
One cannot fill his belly selling pearls of language
Which were snatched out of the flames of life.
In this era of relentless change,
As info-tech dominates human lives,
Some say that robotic poetry is on the verge
Of replacing all the poets of today.
I think not: that would be too arbitrary.
The reason that poets still survive today
Is that their poems come from the soul.
Each line throbs with life, breathes with feelings
Which aren't something a program could cook up.
Even curses are filled with deep-cut hurts.

And so, poets, I have no fear of robots,
But I worry that the day may really come
When we face violence, evil and injustice,
But can only stay silent, lacking words to speak
For victims of war and hardship and disaster,
And failing to lend a precious helping hand.
Lacking sympathy, we may fail to summon up
Words of justice and love from deep in our souls,

And by then, we will have turned into robots…

Translated by Denis Mair

The Secret Language of Poems...

When the Yi people want to purify their house
They dunk red-hot stones into herb-infused water
Letting steamy vapors permeate the interior
To rid the place of impure entities.
Who can say if the hiss of stones does this
Or is it by the power of flame itself? Or does
Another will overcome the boulders of darkness?
I believe in marvels, but not out of superstition,
Because I have seen a priest of my tribe
Clamp teeth on a goat's neck and fling it onto a roof.

Sinful acts are happening every day
In all corners of the globe where people live.
Many heart-wrenching stories tell us
That human morality and noble deeds
Don't arrive with an infant's first wails,
Yet when the mother starts to chant a lullaby
We realize that in her child's unknowing state
The secret language of poetry is being imparted.
Ah yes, those sinful deeds will still be committed,
Yet because of what poets feel driven to offer
This absurd life begins to take on meaning.
As for palpable actuality, it may lead us
Down the road to nothingness.

Translated by Denis Mair

A Poet in His Waning Years

Please forgive him, despite what is etched in his bones
He can no longer utter all their names;
Those bird-shapes vanishing over highland groves,
Their traces gone in gathering mist.
That is an ocean given scope by time;
Sails that dotted it have slipped from sight.
That is a serenade of love songs,
But today only memory, in the form of soliloquy,
Communes with the deathly silence of years.
Of course, certain details still give off flashes
Even now his heartbeat quickens at them;
There is no holding back his brimming tears.

Two lacquer-black braids growing past the rump
And honeyed breath of heart-melting sweetness,
Crystalline eyes like animated pools,
Pink lips on which poetry has suckled,
Ah, all seems to have dropped into an abyss,
Lovely features swept off by an insomniac wind.

Ah, such is our poet, he had love to offer
For poetry's sake, and then poetry offered itself to him.

Please forgive him, he took time to bury bygone things
At the bottom of his heart…

Translated by Denis Mair

For My Father's Generation

People of that era were put through trials
Of raging wind and pelting rain.
In that era's massive transformations
There were new chances and, of course, downfalls.
They were the elite of our tribe,
And those who managed to survive
Were only the lucky portion.

They were favored sons of tradition, well-versed
In mountain language and ancestral wisdom.
They knew the intrinsic meaning of word roots,
Which they served up in rhymes and sayings
On festive and mournful occasions.
While still in middle age they made ready
Their own coffin and burial clothes.
They had passion for life, without fear of death.
They were lead figures at holidays and parties;
The reputations of their mounts were known afar.
They defended dignity and cherished honor.
Some of them, to prove the value of living,
Did not shrink from giving up their lives.

Compared to them, we have visited
Many more places in the world,
But when we attempt to sing
Of native ground, then we realize
They were more powerful than we are.
We have lost ourselves, and in our dreams
The ranged mountains live no more…

Translated by Denis Mair

My Sister's Woolen Cape

If blackness were to encounter love
Most pure in its excess, adrift in the night sky
Of fathomless indigo, ah, sister, could that be your dream
Or myself as you've dreamt me? I don't know who created
This reality more distant than fantasy.
Could it be a miracle that came to pass in childhood,
Reappearing as an echo in this moment?

Forgive me, I can't call the incident to mind
Yet I see you wearing that woolen cape,
But it's just a figment, no longer mine,
Seen by someone else, in an eternity of forgetting.

Translated by Denis Mair

Jaw Harp Master
—*For Edi Rihuo* [1]

[1] Edi Rihuo is an heir to the Yi Minority's musical heritage. He lives in Butuo, deep in the Liang Mountain heartland.

Is your secret code only to be understood
By the lover you pine for?
Does your twanging reed capture a lovestruck
    heart?
Ah, listen! You have fully revealed
The most universal truth of the two sexes.
As the piece ends, your mouth grins widely
Flashing satisfaction from two gold teeth,
Whether on a midsummer evening
Or around a hearth on a long wintry day
The jaw harp calls out to this world
And gathers in each and every response.

Each time Edi Rihuo strikes up a tune
It is like a love affair,
But when love truly comes, only one person
Will know the code of his heart's voice.

Translated by Denis Mair

Indian
—*For Simon Ortiz* [1]

Simon Ortiz said to me: "To them,
We are Indians, but I tell them
We are Acoma…"

Indeed, before they supposedly "discovered" you
You had dwelled in your ancestral place for ages.

All that time, light flashed in the sky's eagle eye;
The root of fertility surged in the earth;
The sun in the firmament passed over a bronze backbone,
Time stretched huge arms towards the horizon's end…

Back then, gods had made a prophecy,
An eagle's return would bring good tidings,
And a chant in the dense pre-dawn gloom
Would revive an extinguished star.

An ear pressed to the earth's chest
Would hear a bison herd's thunder approaching,
Making the earth's womb tremble with thirst for blood.

Atop a bluff defended by ranged mountains
A chief would meet face-to-face
With sun
With moon
With the starry sky
With rivers
With boulders;
Words made poetic through fiery ablution
Would tell his descendants
That this land is theirs.

---

[1] Simon Ortiz, born in 1941, is one of the foremost living Native American poets. He has been termed a leading figure in the Indian cultural renaissance, and has received a Lifetime Achievement Award from the Indigenous Writers Association.

Simon Ortiz, no need to proclaim
That your people are not Indians.
I have heard that the land's memory
Goes far beyond human history.
The globe still spins, and all distorted truths
Will be restored by the land's memory;
The sacred sun—that impartial judge
Will render a verdict in the courtroom of time.

Who can claim to be at the world's center?
We must never believe the conclusion they have drawn.

Translated by Denis Mair

The Ruins of Nizi Malie [1]

No sign is seen that this was once a thriving place;
Hardly a rustle is heard from the cornstalks in ear;
The lane across from the ridge is choked with weeds.
We have not come to rouse our long-sleeping ancestors,
But because we are drawn to our native ground,
Our longing and love for it are etched in our bones.
In accounts of migration, as told in ancestral epics
Many passages give a sense of fate's impermanence.
No wonder, when we set foot where they dwelt
A feeling of hero worship often comes over us.
Ah, sunset silence—the grand sigh you heave surpasses
Blood from the stabbed neck of an offered bull.
We know that none can resist material destruction;
Laws of nature guard the defile where life meets death;

Thus I find something laughable in life, when compared
To death's seriousness, and what we know of death
May be our supposition, while certain rituals—
The ones we are versed in—belong wholly to another world.

By no means should you say this
To one who lacks a sense of humor,
Because there is a legend of death
In which we can find a name like his.

[1] Nizi Malie is the name of a historical site in the native district of the poet's mother.

Translated by Denis Mair

Once I Saw…

Once I saw, in the heartland of ranged mountains,
A Nuosu priest brought a ritual to completion.
Though his voice was a gravelly baritone,
It could penetrate all things, pervade sky and earth.
Such a picture is ever-present in my mind's eye:
It is a prayer for blessings, not a curse;
Firelight and blue smoke take a message to all deities;
Phantoms from a drumskin float across the sky;
Chanted tones sink slowly into the infinite.

Violence is not elsewhere—it follows humans
Into so many places; just yesterday
It snatched the blood of a child in Syria.
So-called "justice" and "rights" may just be words
To which people pay lip-service in manifestoes.
Yet when prayers for blessings are said in various ways
We should accord them fitting esteem:
In that moment they allow us
To look beyond the sufferings of this world.

Translated by Denis Mair

Poet

A poet is not a magnate of commerce, nor is he
A hyped-up figure on TV or other media.
He need not pay hacks to cook up lurid stories
Or clash with fake opponents on the Web,
Or resort to ruses to generate a buzz.
The reason poets exist in the present day
Is that words they write are not exchangeable
For money, because every word
Transcends the value of material things.
He is not a superman of the entertainment world;
He cannot throw away the key to his heart;
He wanders between city and countryside;
He is a chief of the last tribe; he uses
Rare metals of language to toll the bells
That hang in the tower of an ancient city.
The poet is a lone mustang; he does not run
With horses kept by any herdsman,
Yet he always stands in their vicinity.
A poet is not suited to a role in a choral troupe:
He would rather sing in solitude.
Amid the crowd, the poet is a tiny minority,
Yet he chooses to stand on the side of the weak.
Although he suffers the blows of malign fate
He will never give up his spirit-protecting talisman.
Among birds, the poet is of the omen-bringing kind;
He is the earliest cuckoo foretelling spring.
He stands on a peak he himself erected,
Releasing his storm of thought into the cosmos.
Some say that poets themselves are a social class
Scattered in various corners of the globe.
O azure vault above, let them survive

For they would never ruin language;
Still less would they despoil life.

Translated by Denis Mair

Jewish Graveyards

There are Jewish graveyards: I have seen them
In Warsaw and Bucharest and Prague
And in Budapest. For a strange reason
They made a huge impression on me.
Were they the layouts? Not exactly.
Were the different settings? That wasn't it either,
For Europe's graveyards don't have major differences.
Later, without much thought, it dawned on me
That other places were unkept, with weeds to be cleared,
But they were not as bleak as that Jewish graveyard.
Around me were leaning plaques and sunken graves;
Blackened moss covered a lane leading to its recesses.
I feel that death will happen to humans at any time.
It is good for survivors to find an outlet for grief,
To visit the grave and call up memories of the dead.

In Eastern Europe I saw many of them—
Those Jewish graveyards so bleak and deserted.
"Why is that?" I asked the guide who was with me.
After a short silence, he said in low tones:
"Their relatives all went to Auschwitz [1]
By one-way ticket, none came back."

In Eastern Europe, there are Jewish graveyards:
I saw quite a few, and only then did I know
Heaven may only be in our imagination,
But Hell trails our steps like a shadow.

[1] Auschwitz: A death camp built in the polish town Auschwitz during the Nazi German regime, on which about 1.1 million people were killed, among whom most were Jews.

Translated by Denis Mair

José María Arguedas [1]

My blood came from huge boulders; by their strength
My ribs support the revolving bodies of heaven;
But with a lance's swiftness
The shadow of the sun
Descends upon holiday flowers.

I am José María Arguedas,
A Quechua of Peru, a typical native.
My modes of thinking and acting
Do not fit in with those of others,
Because I believe that our way
Is not the only way.
Only through differences we can find
A way to tolerance and understanding,
And so I intend to defend it:
This way of ours,
Even at the cost of my life,
I will have no regrets.

My frame was clad in llama wool,
In Andean pastures abuzz with bees
As the male eagle paused
In the silence of time
And wind
Blowing upon
The invisible pan-pipes
Of our life-force. That is our voice
Which has passed
Through uncounted centuries.
It has borne witness
To blood,

[1] José María Arguedas, born in 1911, was a Peruvian Indian novelist, anthropologist and defender of Indigenous rights. He committed suicide in 1969.

To birth
And destruction.
That is the sound of our river,
Its profundity and freedom
Were what forged the souls
Of the sons of the People.
Because of this…
We have chosen:
To live on this piece of land,
To die on this piece of land.

Ah, friends of the future
This is not my testament,
I am not that fox on the hill—
While running it looks like flame;
I am not that fox below the hill—
Its yelps strike sorrow into human hearts.

I want to tell people this:
I, José María Arguedas
Did not die of poverty
But of suicide,
For no other reason
Than my unwillingness to see
The death of my tradition
In my own lifetime.
It was for no other reason…
Not a complicated matter.

Translated by Denis Mair

Juan Gelman[1]

In a poem you spoke of me
Throwing words into a fire
So that fire will keep blazing
In the house of naked language.
As for you, you kept throwing your death
Into life and into fire.
You know about the causes of evil;
Most importantly, your voice
Shook up the world of death.
You would never have cursed life itself,
You took fate's malignity on yourself.
On the day you departed, it is said
In Mexico City, a leaf from heaven
Finally fell onto your empty shoulder.

[1] Juan Gelman (1930-2014) was a contemporary Argentinian poet and one of the foremost figures of Latin American poetry. He was recipient of the 2007 Cervantes Literary Award.

Translated by Denis Mair

An Alternate Explanation of Freedom

Let us celebrate yet another liberation of mankind,
As it soars boldly across the open sky of will.
Using machine-extracted data you will read me,
And to you I am no more than a moving location.
My sweet words no longer belong to one person,
If needed, all of mankind can enjoy them.
Whatever happens in the world today,
All of us can find out right away,
And I could be anyplace on the globe.
Dear ones, thank heavens, please feel at ease:
You can be done with me anytime you want,
Then go on to play the next cat and mouse game.

Translated by Denis Mair

Great River
—To the Yellow River [1]

[1] The Yellow River, China's second largest river and fifth largest in the world, originates on the Qinghai-Tibet Plateau. With a total length of 5464 kilometers, it enters the ocean within the borders of Dongying, Shandong Province.

Up in a higher place, where light reflected from snow
Subsides into depths of time, that is a tabernacle
Of the gods, where a solemn, even-toned chorus
Resounds upon a brow sequestered like gold ore
As yet unnamed, no fixed meaning inheres there
Its sole death is none other than birth,
Its countless births none other than death.

Meantime, light the envoy takes a stance at the land's center
With a pure gaze that cannot but change into embers of wind;
Once the name is given, a carnival of all beings, on the plain of gods
Pipes a tune that animates an ever-unfolding ground-stuff
As dawn's veil parts over rangeland of boundless ochre;
Light flashes on an eagle's wings, casts their shadow on the earth,
All prophets stoop at the entranceway of origination
Waiting to be crowned, ushered by sunbeams and flames
And in a white riverbed, like a voluminous tableau
The sky's altar ascends, the milky way of gods manifests.

Meantime, sound circulating in obscure muteness
Rouses a great sea, deathly and yet alive.
No need to crouch down, the heedful ear discerns
An untiring clamor, remote of source but not vacuous
From the sacred theater of gods, prior to creation
The legendary Twelve Tribes of Snow take birth,
Their spirit and flesh cohering, never opposed and warring.

The salvation of life begins far from here and now
When heads are shaded by shadows of snowy peaks.
O Great River, before you appeared, all was blank
And the Word alone was sole truth, only thenceforth

Could iron abloom with longing, held by us
    and all our relations,
Change to garlands of equipoise, down to
    future generations
Frigid emptiness, slumber in whiteness, abyss
    being toppled
Bird of stone, another kind of face, ever-
    unsettled daylight

That time had no rulers, only stirring wind
    and passing fire
In company with Being—vast and limitless,
    desolate and immense
Who was true sovereign here? The figment
    that created everything
O Light, omnipresent light, which alone is the supreme ruler
By light alone could ethereal air be enkindled to dust specks
Light is the backbone of heaven, it is the lance of the cosmos
O Light...light is a heart pumping itself, a boulder as buoyant as
    feathers
Pouring through airspace of the sky-vault...like a cataract in free-fall
Upon light's appearance, sun and stars, such pure entities
Bear witness to a grand ceremony, O Light, because of you
In an abstract yet luminous consolidation I first saw water

From there you issued forth. Bayankela[1] created you
Just imagine, one drop of water, a mirror in cyclic circulation
Radiance mottled like agate, going into entities that vanish in a trice
Or distant concretions of ice, maiden-like in their purity
Just imagine, which single drop first foretold such outcomes
And first pounded the door of water's blue kingdom?
Gestation in seclusion, sap of maturation, heat of fertility
As the eagle's nest and gateway of legend light up totemic emblems
The placenta of earth is sucking and quivering and conglomerating
Water of Zhaqu, water of Kariqu, water of Yueguzongliequ[2]
And all those filigree lakes strewn like turquoise stones

---

1 Bayankela is a mountainous area at the source of the Yellow River. In the language of local inhabitants, its name means "opening in rich mountains."

2 Zhaqu, Kariqu and Yueguzongliequ are the first three source streams of the Yellow River.

This territory of whiteness has no near shore or yonder shore
It has only water's thinking—corolla of a flower that climbed a
    railing
Each birth that takes place is a magnificent nativity
Like a revelation, in which that remote echo is heard
Here there is only stone, volition has not taken form
With an inner core emitting coded suggestions of darkness
By virtue of height alone, each drop of water amazes us
Thousands of veins slurp down its colorless balm as yet unfelt
Soliloquy of antelope, arc of snow leopard, horned bellow
At a storm's apex, shaking awake the drowsy messenger

O Great River, nobody can give you a name
Because your very color gives utterance to your name
On your arms grow fields of golden wheat
Stars poised on high stir winds in herbage-scented air
Yellow mud is molded into dazzling bodies
Dancing men and women disappear at midnight
Yet gain lasting life on swirls of painted pottery
Water allowed their hands to feel the touch of dreams
Enabled a maker of offerings to grasp the fire within ice
By dawn's first light, in children and livestock and smoke
Whenever eyes opened, a mask of god might appear

O Great River, before your words were spoken as words
You never told us of your past lifetimes
Once your words were spoken as words
You never revealed your mirror's obverse
Your confiding murmurs moved spirit-endowed creatures
Yearning lips were dotted with fir trees and bracken
You are the primal mother; once you were an infant
A protective cradle of mountains witnessed your growth
Divinely inspired epic, with ritual implement in hand as key
When your lustrous hair was combed by wind at dawn
Your girlish poise commanded the glances of gods
Such dazzling beams were enough to blind all gazers
That was your blue era, time of overpowering beauty

Declaring that truth is another suppositional quality
If knowledge of your girlhood years were to slip away
We and all others who give you the title Mother
Would be unworthy and unfit to be your progeny
In your motherly image, you have long stood before us
Like a megalith, not to be shaken by anyone

We give you the title Mother, whose dark nipples at dusk
Were broached countless times with sssp-sssp-ing sounds
On the naked body of the good earth, our rhythm
Is the rhythm of waves, the rhythm of flowing water
Along with seeds in springtime we make lucid vows
High skies of autumn in time show scenes of fruition
Before the dark of night comes, a boundless weariness expands
Like returning sheep, as yak chips glow ruddy in a fireplace
This is the lane of freedom, from yurt to mud-brick house
Where dreams like stones climb to lofty vantage points
Children sleep under fur robes, and autumn leaves sway
In windy treetops hung with stars and moon for lamps
On this high plateau dreams extend in surreal directions
A music is made in patterned moves and breaths of creatures

O Great River, deep in the yellow earth along your banks
Are buried many heroes and wise ones, their silent bones
Once raised the banner of justice, stirred storms of wrath
Had all this never been, mortal oaths wouldn't have been cast
Toward latent fire in tones of bold, sorrowful, plaintive songs
Earthen walls of uniform color having fallen, new earthen walls
Were raised by other hands, but enduring spirits of forebears
Abided and passed through a millennial caravan with its livestock
Witnessing ancient death and new births that were surely no novelty
On this stretch of land dwelt people who were silent and voiceless
When the tempest came, raining blows of unheard cruelty
On body and beloved ground, testing every ounce of mettle
They succeeded in holding back the rapacious enemy
In stories thereof, handed down from living memory, the narrators
Are like those who tell of heirlooms with their warm auras

O Great River, your language outdoes gold and precious stones
On the tongue-tip of your poet, the jolt of mysterious force
Accesses secret word-strings, stepping up a naked tension
Behind kindred entities, generating life among substances
Facing those whose intoned words prove to be undying
Whether of the millennium past or the millennium to come
We feel the weight and luminosity of their abundant fruits
And that is you, altering your form of existence in reality
In this world, no other river touched by the god of poetry
Resembles the poetic canon you lent yourself to
The moat of words you have built is still unrivalled

When we bend toward you, to receive salt and hourglass sand
An unseen hand passes through a glinting needle's eye
That is your original water, newly discovered and verified
It takes the mother tongue's indeterminacy to reach that pristine spot
Or this may be the crowning vantage point of Oriental civilization
It is the magnetic red spot at the center of a geomancer's dial
By tolerance of otherness, it widens the creases in iron
In the place closest to you, those diverse ethnic groups
Identify with co-existence, oppose division, guard tradition
In different languages they describe the brilliance of sunset
In that faraway place, nestled high among ranged mountains
When freedom blows hither on a wind from depths of the cosmos
All alone, you eschew your mask of sacred yellow
So freedom's color can weave the future's sky-canopy
So extinguished lamps can be relit by the sun
So a fertile womb can bloom with scent of osmanthus
So a thousand grain mills along with timeworn millstones
Can grind and rumble through piles of grain on plazas
So firewood in stove-bellies can burn more hotly
Casting red light on farm wives' faces for years to come

O Great River! Your two banks, aside from growing crops
Nurtured generations of singers, each worthy of renown
Each in different vocal tones put this world into song
Into songs needing no translation, only a heedful heart

They have power to move listeners time and time again
You make singers forget their lot in life, forget themselves
On this planet, you are the navel of the Orient
Through your vessels trickle different types of blood
Yet all are red, and this color belongs to you alone
You are not a single person's memory, if anyone's—
You can only be found in the memory of millions
Yes, it is collective memory, the memory of a people

When you were still a single drop of water,
Still a tiny portion of life within an embryo
When you were still an unseen entity
Not big enough to be discovered by us
When you were just a word, an opening
Not having assumed the proportions of an epic
O Great River! Did you hear the call from the ocean?
Likewise, Great Sea! Across your unbounded reaches
Freedom is the very element of your esteemed soul
Embodying justice, you defend life and human rights
Only for such causes will poets of various mother tongues
Do their utmost to praise your glory in their verses
Yet at this time, Great Sea, I have to ask a question
Amid your ever-surging swells, when rays of dark-matter
Beam down on you from black holes of the cosmos
When weariness follows your tides and a huge, dark stillness
Occupies the many dimensions of space and time
When whiteness flies like banners from masts, resembling
Thousands of seagulls in a wheeling dance at noon
O Great Sea! At such a time, it is important to know
Have you called out to that original, single drop?
Have you heard the first note of the piping of Heaven?
Do you know the first word spoken by the creator?

All such things are possible, because this watercourse
Has already told us its entire secret history
It is real, just like the land it moistens and nurtures
On its banks we work and sing, life always engenders life

Through generations, welcoming births, dying placidly
It grants us life's gifts, quiet days, joy and acceptance
Now they outweigh by far the sorrow and misery it brings
Without question, this river with its tenacity and earthy goodness
Has imparted to a remarkable but long-suffering Oriental people
A singular wisdom, as well as its moral dignity as part of humanity
It is of the spirit, because the onrush of years has never kept it
From manifesting in our dreams; as hours rush by
It slips into our consciousness; as minutes slip away
It is part of our breath and heartbeat and being alive
O Great River! Allow me once more, with great reverence
And deep sentiment, to tell the world again
Your name of enduring renown: **YELLOW RIVER!**

Translated by Denis Mair

Disputation Over the Flames

I am over a hearth

My other self

Is down in that hearth

It's not that flames have severed me

But that I and my other self

Are engaged in mortal combat

On the battlefield of language

1 In Nuosu mythology, human existence begins and ends in whiteness. Before birth, souls come from a "land of snow," and after death they travel along a white road to the afterworld.
2 The Nuosu people believe in the eagle as a divine progenitor.

Myself:
I am about to return to the source
Behold the whiteness of womb-light[1]
Gleaming from riverine veins
An eagle suspended by its pinions
Swoops from heaven's silent gate[2]
To insert holy branches across the land
As star signs cycle through hidden courses
I shall not truly die
Death is only a ritual
In the shadow of a flying bird
In the core of a rocky spine
Speech sinks into the lonely sky-vault
And my words above these flames
Transform themselves into tears

My Other Self:
Time is perhaps a virtual dimension
Living things by dying bear witness to all
In a wild place…weed-choked and deserted
An anthill shows intelligence that few understand
Within its maze of interlocking rings
All transpires under a monarch's beck and call
Each caste marches in distinct formation

Their rangeland gives them plenty of room
With stores of wealth to fill their treasury
But purely by chance, a passing ox
Smashed their nest with its giant hoof
I don't know if the antennae of ants
Could sense the imminence of death
But this ending, for whatever reason,
Added a dark chapter to that kingdom's fate

Myself:
In the sounds of my mother tongue I return
Beckoned by half-light to that long-missed highland
Amid tall grass, which gives off a milky fertile scent,
Sparks from a fire-sickle[1] fall and smolder
And crept into the deepest roots
Nursing the forgotten code of salt
Advancing in the direction of the Soul Sending Scripture
The bimo-priest tells me that the memory of language
Is far longer-lasting than the land's memory
Only back on the rangeland of his mother tongue
Can the poet become a true priest
Whose words stir a river of light in the wind
With divine power that never runs dry
Flames of creation inextinguishable

My Other Self:
O weep for all living things
For brothers and sisters are dying
Every hour of every day
We see the logic of capital and machines
Gaining sovereignty over this world
Every plant on the verge of obliteration
Tolls the mourning bell of this century
Though disadvantaged lives, taken together,
Can raise no more than a muted outcry
Yet it pierces fortress walls of iron
Passing through a needle's eye, into the future

---

[1] A "fire-sickle" is a fire starter used by the Nuo-su people. It is a piece of steel carried in a pouch with tinder: when struck against a stone, the "fire-sickle" produces sparks.

To resound beyond heaven's dome
Do not obstruct this call for justice
It will not be abrogated by any force

Myself:
Strip off my ancient mask
To face this world truthfully
I am the eagle's sole begotten son
We bear patronymic names by tradition
Defense of honor outweighs life
As crows flock and land on our shoulders
The wind lifts our colored tribal banners
Wisdom comes down from our forefathers
Vows to die are passed around with a wine cup
For the sake of tradition's extended life
This was not by one person's choice
In a bull's neck lies our collective strength
In a skull forged by travails of existence
To prevail in the end over nothingness

My Other Self:
On this soil that birthed and raised me
As my plow turns over its living heart
I cannot see any longer
The stain of blood runs from its veins
No earthworm wriggles before my eyes
Tiny nameless lives have been slaughtered
By heartless mechanisms
Which person will repent for vanished things?
Up to now, none accept the burden of sin
Each time a boiled potato is peeled
We remember how the land nurtures us
But as we recite sayings of the old days
We see, through eyes swimming in tears,
That our homeland is already gone

Myself:
To praise all ancient food crops
Is the poet's inalienable vocation
We call bitter buckwheat "Mother"
Because it keeps us alive
Among people of our tribe you can see
A mother chews buckwheat, then passes it
Mouth-to-mouth to the child in her lap
As long as buckwheat grows on highland slopes
Tossing freely under starlight
Its story will be told by our people
It has entered our collective memory
No one can say when praise for buckwheat
First became one of our customs
As luck would have it, this is a mission for poets

My Other Self:
On the wall of my house
I've hung two old-fashioned saddles
One of the saddles is male
The other, of course, is female
When my ancestor went on campaigns
With the male saddle,
The female one stayed to watch his household
Who can explain the basis for this?
The existence of every living thing
Apparently was protected by another being
The destruction of an individual life
Portended ill fate for another life
We cannot witness the death of the weak
And treat it as a matter of no concern

Myself:
Having passed through capital's steel canyons
I hear the plaint of a jaw harp
It is such a thin, reedy sound
But it has a moving language of its own

O, that is the most primal, ancient tongue
Conveying nothing but freedom and love
Plucked straight from the soul
Each note touches the heartstrings
It strikes up a plaintive melody
Able to pierce the heart like a knife
Who can speak the player's name?
He is clearly a divine force personified
If only you can understand its subtle secret
Then you are truly a member of the Yi people

My Other Self:
That is my field of buckwheat
It is memory growing through time
Wind rustles the nodding tips of buckwheat
And up in silvery reaches of the night sky
Where a shadow is demarcated with glints of metal
That is an inverted cradle, hanging in space
Which shakes the hypnotic bell in my hand
Fireflies are immersed in night's sea
The whole buckwheat field rises in flight
It is not easy now to reach a mountain peak
To watch sunset spread its unseen wings
Because in that starlit buckwheat field
One can no longer see that young boy
Who once stayed listening to rustling wind

Myself:
I will inherit my ways
Which are the tradition of the mountains
Which are the key to the fire
Which are the burning proverbs
And which are those in our blood
Since the beginning of the world.
In our souls those ranged mountains
Are destined to become a shadow

When the key is cleansed and purified
One thousand times by flame
Then proverbs become the armor
That flows within in our blood
Emitting sounds of a sheepskin drum
Along the road to our homeland

My Other Self:
Stand high on a fortified tower
Yonder is the rangeland of ancestors
On all sides protected by linked mountains
Brawling rivers race through deep hidden gorges
I make out the sense of their confessions
The crowing of feral chickens
Can be heard in the mating season
The chatter of squirrels imparts secrets
An eagle fixes its stare on a rabbit's path
And on a boulder catching afternoon sunlight
Spotted beetles tug at threads of time
Farther off, along a winding road
A young man in sky-blue pantaloons
Sings a ballad in the high tones of Butuo

Myself:
The river wends its way down the valley
Passing through an ancient language
From within the core of words
It blooms into corollas of bone
Every droplet is gilded
Like beads of softened metal
To which our poems give praise
For that is a moat around our homeland
Not every major watercourse
Can instill such gravity in men's souls
Not every major river's name
Carries such freight of pain in a word
At times, it is not an entity to be known

Yet its scars are clearly visible

My Other Self:
On the road that leads to Jile Bute
There is a tree that has stood for centuries
No one knows the times it's been through
Its existence seems to hint at something
When dawn comes to ignite mountaintops
Rustling breezes stir it into plaintive song
As stars gleam in heaven's clear reaches
Its solitude fills the good earth's cup
Once-lush forests were willfully laid low
Maybe not even for the sake of survival
O tree, you greeted and sent off countless strangers
In their eyes, you were an avatar of divine force
With branches ever swaying in an alternate space
Deep down in our minds, you overcome death

Translated by Denis Mair

Who is Faster, Us or Death
—To all who beat against COVID-19 in 2020

Death is faster than us,
because he took us by surprise
and began to run before the starting gun.
Death! This time he seems faster,
but can he really be the Creator's
most recent creation?
Or is this a severe test
that humankind must bravely face today?
Death doesn't wear an obvious mask,
and this time he can disappear into thin air.
Death is faster than us,
and before the statistics even came out
his evil hand was at work
at his accursed additions!
Death's numbers are still increasing,
as now we hope only for subtractions!
Death has traveled far,
killing the elderly, the young,
injuring our vulnerable children,
ravaging the cities, streets, and parks,
everywhere he goes, he beats black iron.

Death is faster than us,
because he took us by surprise
and began to run before the starting gun.
But this time is just like the last time!
We are competing with Death, and now undoubtedly
it is a life and death competition.
Who will come out victorious has yet to be decided.
Let us knit love into our daily practice,
and send it out to every corner, in the name of humanity.
Let us collect the determination of thousands of people

into a single great life force, and from the dome above
send out a light younger than the ancient sun.
Let us open all the windows and snip our dreams into stars
and again lift up a sky as blue as a waterfall.

You say Death is faster than us, but no!
I don't believe it! Because I can see
that the distance between us and Death is reducing.
Please believe that we will create a new record in this race,
with the eyes of whole world looking on!
Our speed is building by seconds and minutes,
along with the speed of our leaders—and from the first moment
that steadfast, confident, and powerful voice spread
across the nation's land, forests, sky, and oceans,
producing a frontrunner of speed that will always be ahead.
This is the speed of the people, whether in the city or the countryside,
and every citizen will fight in this fight without gun smoke,
while every job is held by someone fearless.
This is the speed of the system, rushing to the rescue with commands
that sent an army of countless heroic men and women to Wuhan.
This is the speed of the collective, and the narrowness and selfishness
    of individualism
has no place here, because the harsh reality
tells us, every single life depends on others for survival.
This is the speed of devotion, a devotion that isn't in declarations,
but in families anxiously waiting for their safe return,
and their daily struggle with Death is fierce.
When the cheekbones groan and fall silent, life and death are thinner
    than paper,
and that becomes the battlefield, where one cannot let up the charge,
as what they and Death vie for is one vibrant life after another.
I do not believe in God, but I believe there are angels among us.
Yesterday one cried as she saved another life,
and even with her airtight protective suit, I could see
the tears streaming from her big eyes.
Yes, in front of the television, we watched countless such eyes
behind face shields, and although we don't know their names,

we can be sure that we will see in each pair of eyes
a people's infinite hope and future.
This is the speed of life, from the country's infectious disease specialists
to regular nurses, from city management to every
sanitation worker who still appears at dawn to scrub the face of the city.
Their respect for life is reflected in every job,
and thanks only to their efforts can we maintain our calm and composure.
This is the nation's speed, or one should say China's speed—
the construction of the Mt. Huoshenshan and Mt. Leishenshan hospitals
wasn't gifted by the mountain gods, and the speed of their construction
undoubtedly aroused admiration and wonder.
Those tower cranes aren't masks of iron, but people's spines,
as they pound nails of hope firmly into the leaden void.
This isn't an illusion, it is the unquestionable reality.
Their construction was like dancing on a knife's edge of death.
On TV I saw the hands of one of the workers and they seemed to be growing bigger,
while the joint where the sky meets the earth let out the low note of a shinbone.
So I can affirm that there are many such brave hardworking hands,
and our happiness, fate, and peace will not be held in anyone else's hands—
those hands, not the hands of Jesus Christ or the Buddha or Allah,
but the hands of a Chinese laborer, coarse and dark, but full of confidence.

We are in a deadly race with Death,
another synonym for the virus.
In a yet unknown time, let us bravely destroy him,
not with crudeness or rashness, but with extraordinary rationality and science.
Let us separate our air currents, the invisible vapors,

but not let it influence the warmth and comfort between us.
In the race with Death, there is a frontrunner, but a pursuer can
    become a frontrunner.
In the race with Death, there are no spectators, we are all
    participants.
It is not a Rubik's cube in a child's hand, in today's China
every street is a wartime trench, every home is a fortress.
Oh, this changing disease, this invisible Death!
You are humanity's neighbor, the shadows' shadow, tailing life.
No one can tell us how long you have existed.
When you revived from your sleep, the red spears of disaster stabbed
    into ribs.
With an invisible dagger you launched your attack on people's weak-
    est area.
Oh, maskless Death, this time you once again use your invisibility
to enter our defenseless, free homes.
Our fight has already begun, and I know it is both a defensive and
    offensive battle.
In our laboratories, our finest soldiers are going straight to your
    heart,
and they will find a weapon that can kill you.
For the rest of us, the red signal flares of our frontline defenses
have already lit up Chinese cities, towns, and schools countless times.
Oh, these are the first parries in a people's war
fought by 1.4 billion people.
We must persist, because Death is already wearying.
Have patience! Be strong! Only then we can defeat our enemy!

China in the world, the world in China,
when you struggle to breathe, the earth's other half
feels its face turn red as well. There is a sort of battle that has nothing
    to do
with ancient religion, nothing to do with international conflicts or
    politics.
Oh, world! Today China is facing a fight
to protect the welfare of humanity; the rotating earth
is one family, and when disaster comes, there are no bystanders.

Every bit of understanding, help, or even moral support
will give those in need a source of great power.
Oh, world! China has always been a part of you,
she shares in your suffering, and has never refused responsibility for you.
The ancient peoples of the East and their tenaciousness, sincerity, and decency
have always given wisdom and creativity to all cultures.
Oh, China! You have never used your responsibility and undertakings as a badge,
but to protect world peace, your sacrificial guards and soldiers,
and on their blue safety helmets are born everlasting doves.
When the terror of Ebola surrounded Africa, ebony
idols transmitted the news of death faster than a gazelle.
In The Republic of Guinea, Liberia, Sierra Leone,
more than a hundred Chinese medical teams joined the fight,
and working alongside of locals, they stopped the spread of the epidemic.
Despite the great distance, Africa's drumbeat called to China!
We extended our yellow helping hands to our African brothers,
and trust that in the worst of times, we will never think less of you.
This is our practice of internationalism, and our humanitarianism.
It has no color, but when it's present, there is the color of sunshine
and the color of the sky, and of the earth and oceans,
the color of blood, the color of tears, the color of the human spirit.
Oh, world! Join China's fight today
to beat back the virus, China's battle is the world's battle!

The numbers are still increasing, and they are not just cold numbers,
as each number has a life behind it.
Perhaps the panic will spread among us,
or perhaps you will find yourself panicked in temporary helplessness.
Oh, friends, comrades, you must believe in our collective power,
but we must also remember our individual responsibility.
Oh, Death! He boards airplanes, boards high speed trains,
boards all kinds of vehicles, but friends—
have you realized?—Death is often following us.

Don't give him an opportunity! Wear your masks,
as a single soldier launching an attack, a personal battle,
and only when everyone has become a soldier
will we finally have the magic weapon to defeat Death.
Block him! Hit him as hard as you can! Don't let him breathe,
don't give him a chance to attack our skulls or arms,
as he looks for tiny openings where we let down our guard.
Oh, friends, comrades, if there is an opening,
our losses will be hard to measure,
and more lives will be pulled into Death's orbit,
and those we love will be taken from us forever.
Today Death's spirit still travels the earth,
using his invisible head to beat against every window,
his mouth making sounds that can only be heard in another world.
He kidnaps the air, manipulates matter, cons his way into the crowd,
and on every part of us that can be touched he conceals
key after key to hell. He is unquestionably
a messenger from the netherworld, a parasite that destroys life.
Death has accompanied humans through thousands of years of history.
It is a natural fact, an unchanging logic.
But, Death! This time your surprise attack on humanity
is more frenzied than ever before, cutting off lives amid the sweat.
You break apart families, rip loved ones apart, keep those who should
    go home
from ever going back again. Oh, Death! No matter where you are,
we must gather our strength and beat you back together!

Who is faster, us or Death?
Although he began to run before the starting gun—
do you see?—I can clearly see
when the free wind rustles the red cape of heroes, when the sun's
arrows pierce the dark cliffs, when light's liquid reflects back to the
    universe
and escapes the pull of the earth, when women's wombs conceive the
    earth again,
the language of plants becomes triple the glow of fireflies,
when all the animals' eyes can compose multi-dimensional philosophies,

in every person's chest a stalk of lifesaving buckwheat will sprout.
When we each become the other, when we all pay attention to the
    smallest life,
behind every person's voice will be the community's voice, and from
    one person's voice
we will hear the voices of the countless many.
Yes, I can distinctly see, our race with Death
has reached the final sprint, and we are about to overtake Death.
This is the hardest moment, and the one who persists will be the
    hero.
Believe this! We will win! China will win! Humanity will win!
We have already begun to overtake Death!

Translated by Eleanor Goodman

Split-Open Planet
—For all of humankind and all living things

[1] *Chama*: Chamma is one of the ancient epics of the Yi People.

**Did this planet create us
or did we change this planet?**

**O, tigers, with waves rising and falling on their armor,
flowing with the light of numbers. Their sole determination.**

In this moment, they're still in another dimension,
walking alone with the calm gait of Nirvana

That walk which never grows weary, obscure flames.
They make the revolving energy turn into gears, time's
controls hammering the waves of their golden fur.

The tigers are still there. They never left us.
In the four directions of this planet, their toes are treading
on this present about to disappear. Their eyes reflect elements of
    creation.
They don't merely live in the ancient records of the *Chamu*[1].
Their eyes have always been watching a humankind preoccupied
    with good versus evil.

It isn't that every person has committed a specific crime. Once the
    sky begins to hang low, the flight of eagles never again attains
    sufficient height.

As soon as the sky is no longer elevated, consciousness and values are
    destined to slip down from lofty heights. Beside them are injured
    eagle wings.

When the language of sages was sullied by money and materialism,
    twenty years ago, I saw a bird in the city fall to the ground
    from a black chimney and die. Should we forgive the bird or

ourselves? The sky's stillness provides the answer to all.

"It's said that every omen will be transmitted
in a different way." A bimo[1]-priest from
our tribe once stated.

[1] Bimo are the priests who pass on the written language in the original Nuosu religion.

This war has finally arrived in a manner
invisible to the naked eye.

O, ancient foe. Who intruded on your homeland, using offend as a
metaphor,
as if this could alleviate some of their sins? Yet, without a doubt,
it was humankind who roused you from a slumber tens of
thousands of years long.

From one city to the next, from one country to the next,
it crosses traditional boundaries even though there are soldiers there
armed to their teeth.
It crosses over sovereign territories, because no one can stop the free
flow of air.
Even the most advanced probes didn't detect its peculiar
whereabouts.

This is a unique war, a different death metaphor.

Of course it doesn't need a passport; it can go wherever it wants.
You see migratory birds that fly in accordance with the seasons, fruit
bats hanging upside down from cliffs,
red-bottomed orangutans chasing those of the opposite sex, insects
jumping across species;
they all throw the dice of life and death toward the mailboxes of
heaven and hell.

It visited churches, mosques, Daoist temples, Buddhist temples, and
secular schools;
It struck open nursing homes on lock-down and heavily guarded
prisons.

If it can it will rouse every government in the world. The mask of the
    god of death
will nail black panic into space. The red spear will kill the black
    shield.

When the East and the West meet again at
    Fate's exit,
are they leaving dire straits? Or annihilating
    themselves?
The left hand blaming the right hand can't
    build
a new Noah's Ark to escape the plight of these thousand years.

The lonely planet is still spinning, but a prophet will always appear
    among the twelve sons of the snow peoples,
since *Le'e*[1] tells me all animals and plants are brothers.

Although the seas Homer chanted of are still surging liquid blue, the
    eyes of seals are filled with messages of the universe.
Perhaps this isn't the last judgment, but the bowl-shaped blue heavens
    covered
the heads of humankind before unicorns appeared.

This isn't a traditional war; it's even less of a nuclear war; a nuclear
    war has no winners.
Marie Curie spoke out for a just political regime. Even now we have
    no way to judge if she was right or wrong,
but thank heavens her conclusions concerning nuclear weapons
    haven't elicited slander or controversy.

This is a reappearance of wars that have appeared before,
but it's even more dangerous and frightening
since the global village of today is a double-edged sword for
    humanity.

A war is so ancient yet close by, no one can remain beyond it.
It invaded formidable dynasties, and rewrote the history of ancient

---

[1] *Lei'e* is one of the ancient Nuosu epics passed down in the Yi areas of the Greater and Lesser Liangshan Mountains.

imperial Athens.
In the Middle Ages, it effortlessly annihilated over a third of Europe's population.
It was also the colonizers' accomplice, killing hundreds of millions of Indigenous Americans.

This is a war of resistance that belongs to all humankind collectively. It doesn't distinguish between regions.
If I could, I would choose to protect every single life,
not to use abstract politics to interpret the connotations of so-called freedom.
I think Adorno[1] and the poet Ernesto Cardenal[2] would approve, because
even the humblest lives are greater than vacuous preaching.

If public security is constructed by each person,
I'll choose to obey the collective and not to resist.
From Wuhan to Rome, from Paris to London, from Madrid to New York,
we can see gazes on balconies that are familiar to us yet belong to strangers.

My respect for individual rights is based on respect for the rights of the whole.
If individual rights can harm the benefit of the masses without just cause,
I'll ruthlessly remove these words from the code of rights.
But please believe I'll uphold true human rights throughout my life,
and individual rights are the most sacred element we need to protect.

In this moment, humankind can only cross
this darkest canyon by working together.

O, Benjamin's[3] passport failed; he exhaled on the other side of the

---

1 Theodor Adorno (1903-1969), German philosopher and sociologist.
2 Ernesto Cardenal (1925-2020), Nicaraguan poet, priest, and revolutionary.
3 Walter Benjamin (1892-1940), German philosopher, Marxist literary critic who committed suicide in 1940.

border and waved to me.
In reality he didn't need to appear in my dream to tell me why Stefan Zweig[1] committed suicide.

Fundamentally speaking, his despair
    towards humanity was that he believed
    wickedness had already won and
    couldn't be changed.

O, Euphrates, Ganges, Mississippi, and
    Yellow Rivers,
and all the rivers whose names I haven't
    listed here,
you've witnessed humankind's enduring
    lives and histories; can you
tell me when you swallow adversity, how you
spit back knowledge of survival and shiny,
    unadorned stones?

When I see Dante's Italy inundated with cries at the gates of hell,
Cervantes's descendants are experiencing even more physical and
    spiritual pain;
humanitarian aid is a virtue, no matter where it comes from.

The progress made this century in the fights to overthrow fascism
    and end racism;
Palmiro Togliatti[2], Pier Paolo Pasolini[3], and Antonio Gramsci[4]
    waved Red flags at the cemetery.

In Iran, when people are suffering a double disaster,
those assaulting them have never wanted to let them go.
In times like these, how can I read mystical Sufi poetry,
and how can I not mourn the children suffering in Syria?

Only lies make those who perform before the camera
to get elected truly believe themselves.
It's not that we shouldn't believe their declarations possess true logic,

---

1 Stefan Zweig (1881-1942), Austrian novelist, playwright who committed suicide in 1942.
2 Palmiro Togliatti (1893-1964), one of the founders of the Italian communist party, and an international communist.
3 Pier Paolo Pasolini (1922-1975), Italian communist poet, film director.
4 Antonio Gramsci (1891-1937), founder of the Italian communist party, Marxist theorist.

it's that we should look at how many crimes they've committed
   against the weak.

Now I see a lone sheep in the desert at
   sunset;
I don't know if it was lost by a Jew or an
   Arab.

**Biashylazzi's[1] fire pit, center of the
   world,**
**let me return to the homeland lost in
   your memory**
**through the names of the most ancient
   plants.**

In the distant, arid lands of the Mexican highlands where water is
   scarce
Juan Rulfo[2] is still there keeping watch over his coffin.
In order not to speak, this habitually silent village leader
even turned a parrot into a capricious swindler who could talk.

My true spiritual brother, the world's César Vallejo[3],
you weren't writing poems for one person, you were singing for a
   People.
Let a rooster play the backbone flute in the crop of your language,
and let the poor from every era eat enough before they fall asleep;
   don't let them
only see white milk and freshly baked bread in their dreams.
O, comrade, your alpaca-like simple warmth came from your soul.
It's no secret the origin of your words was 206 pale bones.

**O, civilized and uncivilized. Development or retreat.
   Adding or subtracting.**
—This is a split-open planet!

Here, currency and the internet link all peoples together. Even in the
   most

---

[1] Biashylazzi was a famous ancient Nuosu Bimo priest and sage who passed down the written language.
[2] Juan Rulfo (1917-1986), Mexican novelist and anthropologist.
[3] Cesar Vallejo (1892-1938), Indigenous Peruvian poet and Marxist.

primitive tribes of the Brazilian rainforest, there are people playing
　　killing games on their cell phones.

Bedouins have built an imaginary desert in the city and can no
　　longer see
　　the stars you can reach out and pluck with your hands.
The gypsies in Europe who ride the night lay in the darkness of
　　Europe's cities; they are invisible during the day.

Here, humankind has become the master of all living things, having
　　begun to occupy the territory of the ant king.
Mating Guinea baboons bare their teeth at the people watching
　　them with baited breath.

Here, smart engineering can make the future return to the past, and
　　can make the present become the future.
Ice flames igniting a winter sky are no longer a surprise.

Here, Indigenous women from all over the world just happen to pass
　　through the maze of the internet wearing refashioned hats.
But when they smile at strangers, they still maintain the custom of
　　covering half their mouths with scarves.

Here, half the British are joking about **BREXIT**, and the other half
　　are paying the price of this joke's not being a joke.
This is akin to how beer bubbles turn into smiling tears.

Here, in order to protect the glaciers in the South Pole from melting
　　any faster, dolphins protest by committing mass suicide,
　　rejecting humankind's visits to the glaciers.
Wherever people's footprints are rare, the slaughter hasn't yet begun.

Here, when the snow line on the polar region moves upward, the
　　water fowl on the lake send news of the rising water level to
　　officials with slippery thinking.
And now falcon tears are eggs in the sky.

Here, grains grow in headwinds, hunger has been alleviated, perhaps
 today Malthus[1]
would revise his demographics; his not being a moralist didn't
 influence his existence as a thinker.

Here, the antelope still passes through
 wastelands flooded with sunlight. One
 hint of vibration in the wind will make
 it raise its ears;
sometimes death comes faster than it
 imagines. The bison can't hear the
 discussions unfolding between the
 mosquitoes and flies on its skin.

Here, when New York's streetlights signal to
 turn right, Bolivia's shepherds immediately decide to take the
 small path to the left,
since on the right there are tenacious precipices and a fear-inducing
 bottomless abyss.

Here, Russia's vodka is still consumed the most, but Sergei Esenin's[2]
 lines of missing the countryside
make someone in another country cry silently with grief and sorrow
 after drinking.

Here, Assange[3] created WikiLeaks. As he stood on the balcony of the
 Ecuadorean Embassy and waved to the world,
the death of the poor in Afghanistan coincidentally became known
 to the world.

Here, Catalonians like to eat Spanish ham in the evening, but they
 haven't forgotten
to take care of so-called referendums before eating ham. If Antonio
 Machado[4] were still alive, who would he vote for?

Here, they request the Irish Republican Army and the Basques to lay
 down their weapons,

---

[1] Thomas Robert Malthus (1766-1834), English cleric, demographer, and economist.
[2] Sergei Esenin (1895-1925), Russian lyric poet who committed suicide in December, 1925.
[3] Julian Assange (1971-), founder of WikiLeaks.
[4] Antonio Machado (1875-1939), well-known modern Spanish poet, a leading figure in Generation of '98.

but in other places they issue resolutions supporting separatism.

Here, most Americans believe their wealth has been stuffed into the pockets of the Chinese.
The commandments Moses brought back from the mountain systematically collapsed in the fable of the gene-splicing chain.

[1] Yiannis Ritsos (1909-1990), modern Greek communist poet, left-wing activist.

Here, Guevara and Gandhi were separated and invited into their respective palaces.
The term globalization has been repeated by thousands of people on the double beds at Hotel Elzenveld in Antwerp.

Here, the footsteps of the International Monetary Fund and The World Bank have already walked in places Jesus never went to.
But the poor bearing crosses and walking on the margins of the earth hold steadfast to their belief that Jesus is their neighbor.

Here, some Socialist thinking about labor benefits has been stolen by enemy groups.
Wealth has transcended all borders, but hardship has fallen on the individual.

Here, they overthrow regimes in other countries and create fear among immigrants in their own country.
These cages are so splendid, the poems Ritsos[1] wrote under the prison window have already grown into trees.

Here, television stupefied people into broadcasting live the collapse of the Twin Towers.
In Colombia, poetry has become the most humanitarian means of political dialogue.

Here, each day marginalized languages and lives are quietly removed by controlling powers.
But in terms of personal privacy, 97.7 per cent of the people in the

world are naked under surveillance.

Here, Karl Marx's ideologies are still
becoming concrete movements, but
Wall Street is more willing to conspire
with elite academics,
saying this Jew is only a leader in one
academic sphere.

[1] Jürgen Habermas(1929-), German philosopher, one of the main representatives of contemporary Western Marxism.

Here, some people want to continue opening
doors, but others close the doors that are already open.
As soon as the ground beneath our feet leaves us, distance loses its meaning.

Here, those opening doors don't entirely know what to let in and what to block out.
Some people are in virtual space being deprived of the ability to expand boundaries and receive the same identities.

Here, those who advocate closing doors aren't worried their own houses will one day become cages,
but those who are spiritually exiled from their homelands are eternal targets to be banished from freedom.

Here, the skeleton has already become a whole body. If you cut away one hand it can bear it,
but if you cut the skeleton in half, it will be hard to survive. Shanghai's ears can hear Florida's toes moaning.

Here, the bars in St. Lucia in the South Pacific are still playing saxophones, each soda bottle that's opened can hear the pleasant surprises or sighs of the NY stock market.
Online bullying is the fifth column of the current era. Habermas[1] randomly saw the truth.

Here, people burn down 5G cell towers; this is undoubtedly a foolish medieval reversion.

Even though Australia's red-breasted robin is the last to chirp, its
    chirping is full of speculators' suspicions.

Here, we no longer have the Inquisition
    executing Galileo, but there are still
    people following fundamentalist orders
    to kill infidels.
It isn't that all so-called democracies indulge
    the weak; Jefferson[1] thought that
    eliminating Indigenous peoples was
    great cultural progress.

Here, the ratio of rich to poor hasn't actually
    changed, but class boundaries have
    been erased by new liberalism.
When they need to, a translational government will reconfigure
    depriving the poor into a benevolent act.

Here, not all countries can manufacture a button; of course the
    purpose of this is to enable the button to swim to all places that
    have an ocean.
All those fighting over transforming the world were equal at the
    beginning. No wonder on his deathbed, Trotsky believed in
    arguments for continuing the revolution.

Here, they knocked down the Berlin Wall, but built more walls in
    order to separate. The walls are thicker and taller.
The panoramic prison made opaque space once again descend into
    the inescapable trap in Orwell's[2] *1984*.

Here, debates about freedom and lifestyle definitely aren't about
    racial differences,
since the lockdown brought about by the pandemic isn't for a vague
    majority.

O, split-open planet, did you see the golden tigers spinning your
    body?

---

1 Thomas Jefferson (1743-1826), the third president of the United States, primary author of The Declaration of Independence.

2 George Orwell (1903-1950), original name, Eric Arthur Blair, English novelist and social critic. His masterpiece was the novel *1984*.

Did you see them disappear into the sunrises and sunsets of the vast
 sky? Each breath they take caresses the liquid light above time.
This is the time to save ourselves. We can't make any more mistakes;
 missteps will mean ultimate destruction.

When the signs of catastrophe were sent from all directions
the legendary ark didn't actually appear.
There were no scenes of tsunamis covering one city after the next.
We didn't hear that terrifying sound coming from the heavens.
We didn't witness the mushroom cloud's atomic nightmare rising.
There wasn't one group of countries declaring war on another.
Even though it's not the continuation of the two wars of the twentieth
 century,
the losses and immense damage it creates might be even greater.
This is an ancient, endless war. I say it's endless
because your enemy has been lying in wait for thousands of years.
In the history of catastrophes, you've encountered it countless times.
Goya used his paintbrush to record that the odor of death
was even more shocking than death itself.
It can be ascertained that humankind has entered another dangerous
 arena
and brought a disaster that could have been avoided to the entire
 world.
Now, close-range killing is tragically being carried out.
It doesn't distinguish between countries or races, whether we're rich
 or poor.
When the god of death has just brushed past us, perhaps death is
knocking down a strong man or, in the same instant, pushing over a
 feeble woman.
The god of death, being cursed, has already used intangible violence
 to kill countless people;
among these are whites, blacks, and yellow-skinned peoples,
 including children and seniors.
If we wanted to issue a declaration of war, O, people fighting now,
we would sign this joint name—Humankind!

O, when we step into the habitats where other living beings
 reproduce

at a speed never seen before,
cutting down primitive forests on both sides of the Amazon River in Brazil,
causing a great fire to blacken the green lungs of the earth,
every advancement for the so-called survival of humankind
conceals a mortal danger for the future.
In Africa the popularity of killing wild animals
has caused a constant increase in the number of endangered species.
When the territory of lion-packs is compressed into a pitiful area
the animal at the top of the food chain faces danger everywhere.
Its continuous roars at dusk on the plains
express its indignation toward and protest against the senseless intruders.
In the Third Pole, in the uninhabited region of Hoh Xil,
the homeland the snow leopard watches over is also shrinking.
The carnivores who previously never hurt humans
have started entering villages due to food shortages.
In Southeast Asia, Indigenous peoples have been forced further away by urbanization.
One day a great number of their chickens mysteriously got diarrhea and died.
The death of a child named Kaptan[1] blew an inauspicious mouth harp.
From the Congo to Malaysia when the forest animals are killed
no matter how faraway you are, you can hear the sound of their skulls cracking open.
It's precisely this so-called intimate behavior—hunting and slaughter—
that goes against the mandate of heaven and links these micro-organisms.
In reality, each disaster tells us
we should feel deep reverence for all species.

[1] Kaptan Boonmanuch, born in western Thailand, and died of H5N1 Aviary Flu on January 25, 2004 at the age of six, was among the earliest to die from this new type of human virus. -not quite accurate according to info I found.

We'll pay a price that's hard to imagine
for encroaching upon and destroying even the weakest organisms.

O, humankind, your creation gods have
    brought us miracles.
When Pangu split heaven and earth,
    animals and people walked out from
    the mud.
On the banks of the Ganges, the limitless
    magical power of Lord Brahma[1]
created living things more numerous than
    the stars in the sky.
In the Andes Mountains, the Indigenous
    deity Pacha Kamaq[2]
brought the first peoples and countless birds
    and beasts.
In Greece, where numerous gods resided in
    the temples and heroes came forth in
    large numbers,
Prometheus bestowed humans and visible
    objects with life.
He also offered his own crimson heart as a sacrifice
and finally brought fire, wisdom, knowledge and the arts to the
    human world.
And the son of eagles, our Nuosu Zhyge Alu[3]
made our ancestors' shadows eternally float above the present
    mountains.
Humankind, perhaps your civilization's history may have been cut
    off from that time forward,
but that type of interruption is a mere instant in the long river of
    time.
From the Bronze Age to the age when steam machines rolled across
    the earth;
from the discovery of radium to nuclear energy's benefits to
    humankind being vastly exploited;
from when the Wright Brothers[4] put wings on themselves until
    spacecraft carried people's dreams, one after the next, to the

1 Lord Brahma, the creator god in Hinduism, creator of written Sanskrit checking this with Biplab
2 PachaKamaq, ancient Incan deity said to have created the world.--not quite accurate according to info I found
3 Zhyge Alu, creator hero in the Nuosu epics.
4 Wright Brothers, American brothers Wilbur Wright and Orville Wright, inventors of airplanes. On Dec.7th, 1903, they made the first successful test flight of an airplane in human history.

    distant space station,
computer and bioengineering stepped across the threshold of a century.
We cheered when we saw the black holes in the universe that weren't actually imagined.
The internet allowed us to understand the world anew.
Time and social class, migration and freedom, self and overstepping one's authority, speed and separation,
agoraphobia and one-sidedness, ethnic nations and global views, expropriation and sovereignty,
integration and dividing, bread and ballpoint pens, vagabonds and utopias,
predicted paradoxes and risk calculations, eliminating differences and hostages to fate—
it's precisely because of all these that we gasp in admiration at the setting sun.
Only the thirst for the wonder of the journey and the subsequent probable danger
give us sufficient reason to believe that tomorrow's sunrise will be even more splendid.
But, humankind, without a doubt you are not real supermen; even though you're already formidable enough,
as long as you can't change the fact that you are the existence of this planet,
you will face the same choices all living things face during catastrophes.
This is the fate the gods of creation set forth, no one can easily change this.
That invisible hand made all living things form a crystal circle;
any avaricious destroyer will sink into fear and drown.
All living beings might be carrying their own murderer in their bodies.
Moreover, humankind isn't made of metal, and it has the weakest parts.
We're powerful, so powerful we become the world's dictators.
We're so weak perhaps a micro-organism invisible to the naked eye can defeat us in an invisible battle.

Humans will always be just one among the biological groups;
we don't have the right to ceaselessly expropriate this earth.
Aside from the most basic survival needs, any slaughter of other
    living things can be viewed as a crime.
Treat nature well, treat lives other than our own well, please
    remember this!
Treating them well is treating ourselves well. The alternative is
    eternal doom.

O, humankind, this is the time disinfectants flow along national
    borders.
It's the time when you'll be next if the person beside you gets it.
It's the time when dissolving time and thirsty arrows are in a race.
It's the time when we mock others and can't do good by ourselves.
It's the time when that zealous ice is carving the raging inferno.
It's the time when the earth and people simultaneously don
    facemasks.
It's the time when eagles in the sky fight with red foxes in the
    wilderness.
It's the time when all the boulevards and public squares fall silent.
It's the time when children can only imagine the ocean from beside
    the window.
It's the time when angels in white and the god of death approach the
    abyss.
It's the time when lonely seniors will devour despair in one gulp.
It's a time when it's safer to stay home than it is to go out.
It's the time when the outstretched hand in the throat of vagabonds is
    the hungriest.
It's the time when advocates for humanitarian aid are greater than
    ideology.
It's the time when urban tribal peoples are forced to return to the
    countryside.
It's the time when the earth, sea and sky pay their respects to living
    beings.
It's the time when doves fly out from cut-open veins.
It's the time when Italian tears blur Chinese eyes.
It's the time when moans in London make Spanish guitars whimper.

It's the time when New York nurses cry with God.
It's the time when lies and the truth appear and disappear on the internet.
It's the time when Gandhi's people disturb the faraway elaphure.
It's the time when humankind's glory and evil come face to face.
It's the time when it's hardest to believe the other side or doubt one's enemies.
It's the time when language gives people hope yet provokes hatred.
It's the time when half the people are perplexed and the other half are worried.
It's the time when the breath of blue whales stirs peace.
It's the time when the stars send off the dead on behalf of relatives.
It's the time when a thousand priests curse a shadow.
It's the time when the faces of strangers start to become distinct.
It's the time when people in the same bed with different dreams now dream of each other.
It's the time when people seemingly together but actually divergent start a cold war.
It's the time when the old is on the verge of collapse and the new hasn't yet arrived.
It's the time when the divine branches declare misfortune or disaster will be averted.
It's the time when black stones conceal white meanings.
It's the time when the sheep of all gods are waiting for Moses to cross the Red Sea.
It's the time when the bull-horn blown by warriors tears you up with grief.
It's the time when the eagle goblet is grasped once again by the poet prophet.
It's the time when the people and living things on the Tower of Babel earnestly engage in peace talks.
It's precisely a time like this. It's precisely a time like this.
O, humankind. There's only one chance to end this war.

Did the planet creat us
or we changed the planet?

When the split-open planet spins the wheel on volition's forehead,
all lives will run under the ever-unchanging sun.
The masks on the gods of creation will
 glimmer in the boundless dome of the
 heavens.
That omnipresent light will return from the
 sky's womb into
the dark, pure air of another space, like the
 liquid womb.
That's our planet's, the only blue,
a virgin olive floating beyond the imagination.
That's our planet, a single water droplet that doesn't fall,
the metaphysical gemstone that can't be casually named.
It's a flame not extinguished by life or death, transformed by the
 creator.
We don't need to be mediums, even up to the present,
we can find its genes of its eyes, bones, fur, and blood vessels in the
 earth, oceans, forests and rivers.
That's our planet, it nurtures all lives.
In spite of wars, plagues, disasters or regime changes,
it's never ceased to nourish and be charitable towards life.
When we caress its body, even though it's beautiful as before,
we can see scars on it that break our hearts.
This is our planet, no matter who you are, what race you belong to,
no matter which place on its body you're living in,
we should all gather together for its vitality and beauty.
Saving the planet can never be separated from saving ourselves.

O, goddess Pumolieyi[1], please let me borrow your needle that sews
 skulls,
and that ball of white-wool yarn in your hands, because I want to
 sew together
this planet we've already split open.

Split-open planet. Let us give you Monday from beneath our ribs.
Let them decrease carbon emissions, let the green leaves from the
 Paris Agreement

---

[1] Pumolieyi, a goddess in the Nuosu creation myths, the virgin mother of the hero Zhyga Alu.

block the nostril casting the dissenting vote, turn his face into a cloak.
Let us give the hungry sustenance, and not just give them numbers.
If it's possible, when they awaken, steal away
    the names of politicians,
don't give liars yesterday's time, because
    the audience will be the largest the day
    after tomorrow.
Let us heal divisions, but this doesn't mean
    making things that are irrelevant uniform.
When 44 are hidden in beams of light, the wooden stool that works
    to no avail will cry out.
That's the sailor on dry land. Adam Mickiewicz's[1] secret key
hopes that those who sleep, having lost one job, will wake up to three
    jobs waiting for them.
The people on the streets already know whoever lights the left house
    on fire,
the yard of the house on the right can't narrowly escape. Despair
    makes the streetlamps grow donkey lips.
Let the hunters of yesterday become today's vegetarians.
Every childhood pledge can be fulfilled when their mothers are still alive.
Let the stones of Jerusalem recover future memories.
Let the desert of the Jewish and Arab prophets who've been
    simultaneously buried bloom.
I hope the end is the beginning, and that the empty sea surges with
    pregnant colors.
Let the wood bowl find parched lips, let faith choose its own clothes.
Let languages that can't understand each other address one another
    at the United Nations.
Let the listeners cheer until they become camels.
Let flags of equality hang in windows all over the world.
Let stability and logic have a falling out.
Let every person become themselves, let themselves like that person
    more.
Let convergence abdicate authority to individuality, let the universal
    become equal.
The cracks in stones are brimming with poems.
Let the hands on rocks grab hold of slippery fish.

---

[1] Adam Mickiewicz (1798-1855), Polish poet, revolutionary, main founder of Polish literature.

Let bankers spew out a polygon of regulations.
Let red cover blue, let the blue mouth sing on the red face.
Let that which is about to die out become rational, let the unborn reconcile with the present.
Let all living things jump with joy into the air; there are soft sponges below them.
This planet is our planet, even though it's as heavy as Sisyphus' boulder.
If we can defy gravity and stand in the sky, it seems more like a child's balloon.
Just because we exist as phenomena doesn't mean all humans have learned to think.
The questions this age has given us weren't in the ancient records, we must answer them ourselves.
We don't have much time remaining, since short-sighted people are still quarreling.
This isn't a disastrous era; we don't know for sure that past eras were superior,
since we're unable to imagine the most remote places from the past have become our homelands in the present.
This is the power of currency, this is the power of the market, this is another power's power.
It has no above or below, it only has what's behind and in front of us; only reality itself can reply to its outcome.
This is an enormous shift, it's longer than a century, it can only be calculated in terms of a millennium.
We can't return to the past, because the old houses have all disappeared.
We can't choose to close ourselves off; no matter what material becomes a high wall, it only implies separation.
We can't choose to resist; as soon as prejudice turns to hate, you or I could die.
We don't need to ask those ancient rivers; their sources are full of prehistory's silence.
Perhaps this was the original enlightenment, diverse civilizations in harmony were all her children.
Give up the difference of three and try hard to find consensus among seven; this isn't putting the problem off on others.

Within a square might be a round possibility; it's not being prejudiced
 by first impressions.
Let everyone abandon the laws of the forest; this should be better, not
 viewing oneself as most important.
Let people try to make bright times last longer rather than bestowing
 darkness on each other.
None of this is a simple method; it's making all participants aware
the future of this planet doesn't just belong to you and me, it belongs
 to all lives.
I don't know what will happen tomorrow; it's said poets have the
 ability to foretell the future,
but I won't predict the future, since the boundless oceans didn't leave
 any traces in the sky.
The light I've praised countless times is now on a triumphant march.
I don't know what will happen tomorrow, but I know the world will
 be changed.
Yes! No matter what happens, I firmly and steadfastly believe
the sun will still rise tomorrow, dawn's light will be as before, like a
 lover's eyes.
The warm wind will still blow over the earth's abdomen, mothers
 and children will still be playing there.
The blue of the sea will still rise with dreams and, at midnight,
 become the lovenest of stars.
Most people agree labor and creation will still be the main means
 through which people attain fulfillment.
People will keep living, good and evil will keep accompanying them;
 the struggle between humankind and itself won't cease.
The entrance to time doesn't have an obvious marker.
Humankind, you must be courageously and exponentially careful.

Did this planet create us
or did we change this planet?

O, tigers, with waves rising and falling on their armor,
flowing with the light of numbers. Their sole
determination.

Translated by Jami Proctor Xu

Late Elegy
—For my father, Jidi Zuozhuo Wuhelüeqie

When the phantasmal cradle falls from the sky
a hawk's feather covers time, and your thoughts
slowly turn clear, to an unknown mayfly of stolen time
over the mountains and rivers.

Your body sleeps curled on its left side
like your ancestors, and an ancient death trumpets the return
it is the ox horn of all living beings, and repeats
and repeats, but this time sounds more like an aubade.

Light is the only messenger, and those roads no longer lead
to strange places, instead guiding your goats up those steep slopes of
    grief
those hedgehogs who always stand guard do not call your name
though the other lost half of freedom has been looted in terror
this is the last acceptance, and all the spirits and people will complete
    the final rites.

Don't lose your way, not every road can be traveled
a reminder that these are images that when opened won't be lit by
    stars
and only on your own road you can catch glimpses
of the traces left by the saddle. Inaudible speech commands the false
    shadows
troubling the sleep of the proclaimed nine ancient Yi words before
    dusk.

This is your armor, and who aside from you
would dare come claim it, honor and shouting once made the beasts
    subside
every ear knows of your return, and it isn't the dawn wind
that brings the news, but the armor hung on the walls of the ancestral

room
emitting the strange sounds of stirring
only the secrets of death will continue.

This is your silver crown,
engraved on the center of the sun's waterfall
the wings listen closely to the long-settled
    mountains
and the constellations' hourglass is repatriated
    by a stove of goat bones,
let those who accompany you receive the
    burning red pebbles for the gods
this is a naked territory
and all the eyes can see
the hawk disappear into the firmament, it isn't
    the famous hound of legend
Kemaaguo[1] biting an unlucky animal bone, but rather
the diviner's hawk-talon goblet tumbling from the mountain ridge to
    the valley.

Is it you escaping the fetters of the body?
Or are you declaiming your clan genealogy as a warrior?

The announcement of death often spreads faster
than news of success, and travels farther.

In this place called Jilebute[2] in the Yi language
these mountains were your one cradle and foundation
when the cuckoos call and call in the mountains
those breached hours do not happen only in spring
when the blackness becomes crags, and the roosters crow at noon
terrible red snow falls over Riduliesa[3]
signifying that Death has raised his flag all the way to the top
some say that on this day even if the enemy comes, soldiers cannot be
    dispatched.

This is how centuries of men have died, without change

---

1 A famous dog in the legends of Yi people.
2 A place in Liangshan, the biggest area of China where Yi people live in compact communities. "Jilebute" means "the haunt of hedgehogs" in Yi language.
3 A place in Liangshan. According to legend, it is the cradle of Torch Festival of Yi ethnic group.

but desire must not die as well. Mountain
    deities inspect the holy Mt. Abuzeluo[1]
those who have seen black crows fall on the
    shoulders of their clansmen like in a
    dream
can die in a trial of iron gales, or die guarding
    their honor
or die from ever-changing fate, or die in a
    celestial joke
but they cannot die from humiliating
    provocation, with spit effacing their
    reputation.

[1] A holy mountain located at Butuo County, Liangshan.
[2] A famous bimo (priest) in the history of Yi people in Liangshan.
[3] According to the legends of Yi people, as the place where the souls of the departed belong, it is located somewhere between heaven and earth.

There are many ways to die, but there are only
    two kinds of honor and shame
even today, the classics of the highest Yi priest Hebishizu[2] keep the
    names of sages
and virtuous people, and his vision amplified and illuminated that
    road
although the lost eulogy will be unfolded anew and those who still
    farm
inquire about flashing oxen necks, yet after threshing, the bitter
    buckwheat
will feed a people's children in the harshest seasons.

Oh, returning one! When souls of the departed enter the white
    country
a precipice in the sky slides over the distressed hipbones of the
    mountains
the hatchets of the ancestors unburied the boundary between human
    souls and spirits
come eat some oats in tribute, it is the secret book of the firmament
and Shimumuha[3], the boulder where souls gather, is pried away by a
    weeping spirit-horse.

Those are your hurried footsteps crossing over the human and spirit
    realms

the beeswax in your left ear collects dizzying
> light, your shoulders stitched with
> clamshells
Goddess Pumolieyi's[1] flock are as peaceful as a
> pile of stones at dusk
these are the gifts bestowed by the spirits,
> given to fertile humanity
only worship of the ancestors can put those
> who have passed to rest
you may wear the fine clothes of a long
> journey, but when you begin to race
your bare feet are still filled with the
> wilderness's enormous power.

As the spirits cross the heavens and mountain
> ranges, they refuse to step into
the domain of desire and violence, and only
> three-year-old children
can catch a glimpse of them, with their rough unshod feet.

Oh, hero! I hide your name in light
your life will appear and disappear in the hanging gloom
it is a distant slowness, a Jier[2] for an opened door.

This is your infant suckling at the mother's breast
an embryo of a woman, her beauty coinciding
with memory, a tiny finger setting an earring trembling
beauty among beauties, genuine kin to the Agachamo[3]
and descendent of the clan that crossed the river grasping the
> spirit-ox's tail.

This is your arrow, running across sacred Mt. Yimuzemu[4]
the incarnation of an antelope, you see larch trees playing in the
> winter sun
grateful to the prey you hunt, swallowing ochre famine
you returned to an imaginary pupa, the light-biting wings of childhood.

---

1 One of the goddesses in the creation myth of Yi people.
2 An amulet in Yi language. Each clan in Yi ethnic group of Liangshan has their own *Jier*.
3 According to Yi legends, it is a kind of beautiful bird famous for its long neck and being quick-witted.
4 A holy mountain located at Butuo County, Liangshan.

This is your ladder to the heavens, a wasp nest
    plucked from a cliff
and every little friend opens his mouth and
    closes his satisfied eyes,
happy, and welcoming the golden honey falling
    from heaven.

This is you in the back hill of Dajishaluo[1],
    listening to the wind's story
and hearing the sounds of a sheep slipping
    over cliffs in that distance place
it is the hint of the bridle, where to enjoy a nice
    meal
a shepherd boy conspired to push a sheep over
    the cliff's tray
who can explain the secrets of youth, humans
    are always up to the same old tricks.

This is the first glimpse of love's gifts to the body
discovering the guitar and recorder and the possibility of purity in
    death
the Torch Festival is the scarves and candy of small-trouser-bottoms[2]
    who rekindle the stars' promises
a festival of the eyes and the freedom, the damp resplendent bed of
    the earth.
With your hero's genealogy, you tell them who you are! In the place
    where human nature
ends, you resist the timidity of the body, longing for the immortality
    of the spirit.

Here, the names of fathers and sons guide you, spears and shields
    give you a mouth
no need to discover the truth, the gods are engraved on the right side
    of the dead bark
if it isn't the earth's ashes, then we must embrace the will of freedom
and cheer for Chikeboxi[3]! Mouth harp is the language of poets
and because it exists, love can safeguard nobility, subtlety, and modesty.

---

1 A place in Butuo County, Liangshan. This is the birthplace of the poet's father.
2 The Yi people of the Adu dialect region in Liangshan, since the waist of local men's trousers is wide while the bottom is narrow.
3 The most famous home of the mouth harp, an ancient musical instrument resonating in oral cavity, in the history of Yi ethnic group.

This is the first time you and language came to
    embrace the legend of fire
from Degu[1] you learned aphorisms and how to
    observe the sun and moon
when the river deer on Mabuhuoke[2] deliver
    their tender mating calls
the ancient sound far surpasses the history that
    humans know
at dawn you would always hurry to push open
    the wooden door
and dissolve Erbi[3] and Kezhe[4] in water, letting
    the black goats
and white goats lick the drowsy stars hanging
    between the mountain slopes.

In a dream you accepted the gift from the two-
    tongued sheep Yuegehajia[5]
and its far call made the celestial sphere appear in a bowl of water.

You are lightning and copper bell's brother, are the son of condors
    and amber
you are the chieftan chosen by generations of celestial tiger and
    leopard letters.

Maternal pinholes can see the structure of pain
oh, spirits! Everyone is an orphan,
if you haven't seen it yourself, it must be false,
but true certainty is even rarer. Every people has its own
time of heroes, it's just a question of when.
Your courage and insight cut across an entire region
and the ancestors' protection has always lovingly enveloped you.

This is a great clamor, some say when a mountain deity is wrongly
    killed
it must be paid for with a life, or better yet, the hands of blood
    relatives

---

1 A sage of ancient Yi society.
2 A holy mountain located at Butuo County, Liangshan.
3 The ancient sayings and maxims in Yi language.
4 In the oral literature of Yi people, it is an ancient style of poem composed of singing and talking.
5 A famous sheep in the history of Yi people renowned for its two tongues. Its bleating can be heard from afar.

should sacrifice an ox for him! Encircle him
    in the constellations'
navel, and wail at the life about to end
redeem the final payment
this is the familiar scripture, and the
    inherited long-handled sickle,
it reaped the nights and days of our elders as
    they lay stunned by opium,
now only you know, if you can still survive
people and demons have judged you too young.

This is you climbing a poplar, and with righteous cause
shooting a leopard that threatened a pregnant woman, on its skin
was left a hole like its shortened fate, and for you it laid out
a funereal bed, or perhaps it is the pose of a flame-killer across the
    earth
so long as the mountains remain, the hawks and falcons will glide on
    lit wings
the saddles of warriors will wait, and you will become immortal.

It wasn't in the canopy of stars that you discovered what death is
and rejected fear of decay, it was because of your desire about
    meaning
that you knew why one must fiercely fight that hidden, nameless
    darkness
others did not teach us a way to drift above this land
it is because we created our own festivals, the only weightless time
when we can see the flower of existence, and can,
for the briefest of moments, refuse death.

If holy Mt. Zhekemutu[1] had not given you a mystical power
then the ox horn could not have howled like a storm
you once watched the stars and oats as though they were dewdrops in
    a dreamscape
and the body's sensitivity gave you an awareness of all that will
    happen
that instinct to uphold freedom was well versed in the shifts of the

[1] A holy mountain located at Butuo County, Liangshan.

sun and seasons
and finally chose solid stone instead of floating
    wings.
This is a time of changing orders and principles
everyone must undergo the double trials from
    life and fate
not just a part of what has happened,
    revolution and war
let our brothers and sisters stand firm in rain
    storms and tempests, witnesses to hope
and see their tears, bodies and spirits undertaking the heavy burden
    of heavenly stones
your bare feet were accustomed to thorns, but who knows now of the
    pain of flames
no matter how the chaotic constellations shift between unknown
    words
your understanding and casting aside of things prove you have
    always been Yi.

You sleep deep against the earthen wall, resisting needs not entirely
    human
welding a new reality, giving love to woman and children
you are a free seed, your horse is ever tranquil
when night changes the contours of the sky, your thoughts come into
    their own
matching the eagle and the steed, you are a hero
you grip the sun with your teeth, not disappointing the resplendent light
you and the god of wine were always entangled, you used it to pour
    out your heart
it isn't only you—It has created miracles and destroyed lives as well.

While alive, you chose the place for your own cremation
from there you can see far off toward Zizipuwu[1]
you told your eldest son, the drinking cup will always be passed to
    one who is absent
so many of our elders did not live to your age
all living things will be taken back in, only fire will fulfill its promises

---

[1] A place located in Zhaotong, Yunnan Province. According to Yi legends, it is the place where six Yi tribes formed an alliance and started their migration.

the accelerating stars have not changed the
    anvil's position, your funeral rites
are tomorrow, the faint thunder at the edges of
    the horizon tells us
your clansmen and relatives will weep and
    mourn and see your spirit off.

Oh, hero! When the dawn glimmers off the
    birds' outstretched wings
the light's messengers will stand among the mountains, solemn and
    respectful
like the sun's scholars, they will wait until that certain time
when the sacrificial ox's head reflects the hatchet's image, and the
    ox's hide covers
the masks of grief, this is perhaps the entrance to another life
another return to the placenta of the earth, and death must also offer
    a eulogy
let every person at the rites share the meal
while alive, the deceased often said that this was his final request
to extol your virtue, the women wearing black
speak in turns of your glory, and the ribs of the words
are imbedded into poems, the kinds of emotion found only in the
    marrow
here you will trust in the greatness of the tribes, and the sorrow of
    the departed spirit
will transform into joy, you lie in the embrace of love and affection
and each time the sound of crying marks the wound, hidden blood
will trickle out into the heart of the air, and oh, the instrument's
    string snaps again!
The dead can go on hearing the voices of the living, I trust you are
    still here!
When my married sister says, "Now who will
listen to my weeping?" tears gather in the corners of your eyes
the host and guests use tongues of Yi poetry to determine success or
    failure
addressing when eternal death will arrive in the human world
how do our departed relatives gather in that white world

---

[1] One of the most famous ancient Yi tribes in Liangshan.
[2] One of the most famous ancient Yi tribes in Liangshan.

all living things residing in time are so paltry,
    so trite
only spiritual warriors and sages will leave
    names that live on forever
the farewell banners form a line, like the
    Guhou[1] and Qunie[2]
returning to our migratory history, and oh, the
    spiritual exile continues
the butchering of oxen and goats comforts the
    living, the dead of yesterday and the dead
of tomorrow are not different, but the traces left by death
allow the storytellers to surpass us and quietly enter the compass of
    life and death
there red success is returning, the sky fills with the lines
of goat bones, and today is the day we satisfy the spirits, I trust in this.

Oh, hero! The ancient sun gushes with mysterious rays
the ladder from the mountains and earth lifts in a mirage
Bimo[1] again grabs hold of the staff cast from light
and in the final step, he finds the running water that maintains all
    possibility
the dead is lifted on his wooden bed, swaying as though in the first
    cradle
a body cuddle up to the left, as though still in his mother's womb
this is the last triumphant return, you will enter the oracle's palace
you look at that transparent slope opening into many multi-
    dimensional steps
and on the distant river floats a seed whose position in the universe
    hasn't been fixed
the voices sending off the spirit rise and fall, as though falling from
    heaven
and spiraling echoes seem to come from the unreality under our feet
those seeing you off have no perspective, but Bimo and you can see
that dark road you cannot walk, the road is for the devil.

Walk along the white road, where the ancestors walked barefoot
you will see unreal things be revived in the truth, and the body splits

---

[1] In the primitive religion of Yi people, a bimo is the high priest who is also responsible for cultural inheritance.

a pride of tigers stands in the center of a silver
    eulogy, and time becomes a flower
the trees smile in the open, and the algebra of
    the seventh space spreads on the rocks
invisible fish fly over the river, glass plays music
    on the mountain goats' beards
white and black are no longer opposite colors,
    blue rules
over time, which has just been changed, purple and yellow are not at
    their stations
you see a crevice in the horizon gradually multiplying open,
and there a scroll reveals a reflective page, the floor of the light is still
    rising
pillars announce your arrival, a faded image covers the knees
no need for the law to bind, the whiteness demarcates a new rite.

This isn't the castle from the future, the sutures leave no traces in its
    structure
here there is no war, only millions of zoological gardens that have
    passed through dreams
here there is no sharp silverware, only malleable ladles
here there are no ranks or leaders, only ladders prepared for the Big
    Dipper
clear ideas are no longer for expressed, pearls of language roll on
    naked clarity
no one laughs if you take the wrong bowl, the stars do not yield to
    false artillery shells
here there is only white, any meaningless existence will be destroyed
    in the whiteness
the skeleton of the whiteness has opened, and from afar it looks like a
    leaf in the universe.

Oh, hero! You have been lifted onto nine layers of pinewood, the
    cremation fire
Muqielehe[1], the holy mountain closest to heaven, is the consecrated
    place of our ancestors
on the border of the eternal arena, where only sun and fire can roar

---

[1] A holy mountain located at Butuo County, Liangshan.

    for you
your body is covered by a spotless cloak, the final bond between the
    living and the dead
you can hear it, our shouts in the valley lifting up to the blue heights
humans and the universe singing in a chorus, and the crystal notes
    pour from all the hives
that is the power and mystery of our language, the one thing that can
    make a people cry
it is the tradition of humanity's father, it should pierce through dark
    unadorned space
it has just arrived here, it is you whispering to me, saying that your
    immortality has begun
oh, our father! You are the hero of everything meaningful
you breathed, you lived, you suffered, you struggled, you loved
you can see it, in the gleaming door, your ancestors dressed in the
    finest garments
and the grand ceremony for you comes to the end, and now you are
    in another world.

Oh, hero! It is none other than your son who lit the final flames for
    you.

Translated by Eleanor Goodman

Another Springtime

Another springtime arrives unnoticed
as though the wind informed the animals
in open fields
it stretches out hands that shine like crushed leaves
and uncovers the pebbles asleep on the riverbanks
in traces of dreams from yesterday's season
could they be repeating a trick
the dead grasses and newly emerging insects
can perhaps deduce the processes of life
but that vaulting Uranus remains as it was
even far-seeing people in their brief existence
cannot observe over the years of one lifetime
the change in its position
the cuckoo's calls are sweet and bright
their melody brims with flowing light
red pheasants come and go in the damp underbrush
they are the survivors of uncertain fate
beneath the sun clan members are summoned by the spring
and wave to the earth in tribute
the fertile land longing to bear fruit awakens
this is the springtime of a life
and of course it is the springtime of every life
your arrival is reincarnation's victory!
But still, my springtime
when you quietly arrive
and caress my eyelids and lips
I am moved by life
but my body is filled with stones
in those moments, my silence belongs to me
when I realize that only death
can give birth to this new season
in that instant, not for myself, but for all lives
my eyes fill with tears……

Translated by Eleanor Goodman

Ladle

My ladle[1] is a wooden clock-hand
the stars use its long handle to pry the earth.
Oh, to stretch out to the boundaries of
    consciousness and imagination
for the sake of another hand, the Creator
    lengthens
giving us unimaginably enormous favors.
Ladle, thank you for your contribution, a
    hand reaching to the heavens;
the container of the universe rolls along with the silver mirror of
    words
sucking the teat of light and the coarse gold ground out by ancient
    mills.
invisible spirit branches support the movement of ribs;
above are mountain ranges, clouds, and breathing stars
in the places you wish to go.
The home of buckwheat, corn, potatoes, and turnips.
Without you, these extended meanings would be reduced.
No other of my utensils is as important or as comfortable.
Ladle, forgive me, this is the final farewell
and I will hide you along the spirit road
because of your victorious restraint, plainness, and simplicity.
Whenever a Nuosu[2] hand holds your long arm
the colors reverberating through the valleys will spread across the
    festival finery
enjoying the authentic foods, fine meats, and a first mouthful of soup
the heart is filled with thanks for all living things
and all that is passed down generation to generation by the clan.
You do not belong to me, this is a brief possession
and each time you will carefully prepare
for the arrival of new life.

1 This ladle is a wooden serving spoon with a long handle used by the Yi people.

2 Nuosu is the name that the Yi people of China call themselves. In the Yi language, it means a black people, and the Nuosu venerate the color black.

Translated by Eleanor Goodman

Carriage Outside of Time

Whose carriage draws near,
its wheels making a hollow sound in the deepest dark.
The one in the carriage cannot be seen
only light off the snow illuminates the constellation's secret language.
There are no traces of stopping or standing,
just a steep mountain road, leading to nothing,
as if in an even farther place
hooves are answering eternal time.
No time for thought in that short moment,
this is the beginning of a long winter,
and who knows where the carriage is destined?
The dark envelopes it entirely
and this hurrying metaphysical unknown
is a different abstract nation altogether.
Aside from the revolving breath of the horses,
nothing can fully understand the significance.
The carriage seems to confirm disappeared things,
which gaze at us from elsewhere.
No one tells me whether this carriage's
hurrying is the conclusion of a ritual
or a beginning that has not yet arrived.
I cannot judge if this is a kind of truth,
separated by the flames of gradually fading reminiscence:
it's uncertain whether the carriage's raven-black wings
are passing between reality and a bed of dreams;
only the rivets suspended deep in the clouds
can hear the carriage driver's deep distant
inner clamor and silence.

Translated by Eleanor Goodman

Stone

Those stones
with their sleek full skins
have born the weight
of the spiritual illumination
between heaven and earth.
They fall
on the riverbanks
like stars
standing alone in the darkness.

By day,
that waterfall of light
takes the chain of nothingness
and submerges it in its invisible house.

By night,
beams from caves
pour down,
and fine threads
drip into its invisible mouth.
At dawn,
the swaying wind
turns its inner composition
into a secret dark comedy.
"We cannot go inside it,
we can only ever see its totality."

An indestructible whole,
imagine some bizarre iron hammer chose it,
and in the moment it split it apart
all that it concealed would no longer exist,
just like a sigh of the gods.
Translated by Eleanor Goodman

Firepit of the Earth

Firepit[1] of the earth, you are the sun's
inextinguishable reflecting light.
When the hawk's wings throw shadows across
the mountains' forehead and the fruits of a mother tongue,
the floating flames
were not just lit by a mother today.
Stars spread around the firepit of the earth,
we stand beside it and pass on the secret key to language,
nailing the laws of birth and death
to the eternal darkness,
this is the rule of iron, unchangeable,
spinning through thousands of years,
because the light will lead us across valleys,
having already opened another doorway.
Only one staircase leads
to the holy temple of Entiguzi [2],
where the gratitude and enmity of man and god will be reconciled.
But the earth has another firepit,
from which all the other firepits are descended.
The eyes of those three-stove stones
twinkle in three positions in the vaulting dome,
oh, sun! stove for all of the human race and life,
your gentle light is like the golden fur of a tiger,
your dazzling waves dye the sky with tipsy dusk.
You are the sky's inverted moulting mountains, rivers, and forests,
the untiring ever-vigilant hero father of all things above the earth.
"Between the sky and the earth, our ancestors
said this, a solid wooden bowl is better than a bottomless golden cup."
    We live, and that is our mother tongue still gleaming as we talk.
    We live, and that is our roots still shining in the dark.
    There is no reason for life, but perhaps that is the reason!

1 This firepit is the traditional stove in Yi family homes. The base for the stove is composed of three stones, which are known colloquially as the "stove stones."

2 Entiguzi is a god of creation in Yi myth.people.

Translated by Eleanor Goodman

Give Back to the World

We demand too much from the world,
we must give back to the world.

César Vallejo said that he had eaten
that which belonged to someone else.
He was filled with pain because of it.
Not every person
is so aware.

We are exhausting the earth,
encouraged by the masses
we pull the fish from the sea,
making news out of the lucky ones who escape.
We open the mouths of the earth's wounds
and make them bite down on rocks.
Only rocks can withstand such a heavy bite,
but the rocks' legs tremble,
and their eyes fill with muddy tears.

Today, for their own benefit people seek out
ample reasons
to prove the legitimacy of this overdraw.
Lungs gobble up forests, and in other animals' homes
we turn solid steel bars and cement
into an infertile womb for the earth.
It isn't correct proclamations
that stand on the highest moral ground,
allowing the injured and weak to sink into silence.
There is no other choice,
the snowline is rising, the ice is disappearing;
the hawks let fall from the sky
eggs exterminated by anger.

We come in throngs, more than one person.
We open our mouths, more than one person.
The distant man who hasn't been born,
we have already eaten his portion.
We have already secretly carved up
their myriad things,
and tricked them out of their property.
It isn't theoretical, and it isn't
just a possibility drawn from the data.
Perhaps we can create a new wealth,
but we do not have the right! We do not
have the right to deprive another generation of people and lives
of the spiritual inheritance that should belong to them.

We should give something back
to the earth.
It doesn't belong to us,
it is theirs, even if they have no way
to take the case to today's courts.

Translated by Eleanor Goodman

The Mountains of Yesterday, Today, and Tomorrow

It's not merely
moving history,
it exists in reality,
amid the chanting in an ancient tongue
a gleam amid language
like translucent shining crystal.
They have no name
but in order to name them our ancestors
finally led the roots of the epics
to find eternity in our mother tongue,
and perhaps it clings tight
to this star's closest ladder to the sun.
The wind blown across the horizon
is enough to make the earthen walls' sleep
sink in an instant
into the sacrificed river of dreams.
Yes, they have just awoken,
and sway their napes in the shadow and light,
this is the earliest creator's skeleton
and the nipple it offered us,
and who could forget
how we feasted here
on honey and buckwheat.
Oh, unchanging sun,
you tranquil spinning wheel,
tumbling down over our heads
and falling into the eternal silence
that witnesses every birth and death,
and sees our suffering.
Were you not there, firepit of the sky,
our revelry and festivals
would not light the jewel-like flames

[1] The Yi ethnic group has three subfamilies. Going about their ordinary lives, they wear different types of pants: long trousers, mid-length trousers, and short trousers.

a million times in the night sky.
Oh, eternal flames,
you are the sun's greatest symbol,
the infant's first cry
is covered by your stolen light.
This is not a rite,
but the beginning of a rite,
three rocks, the skull for a Tibetan dance, a revolving cup,
we are so close to the flames,
because only flames
can reveal life and death's
most secret processes in spirit branches,
and take every eulogy through into the firepit
and pass it on to us,
when we stand in close crowds
we become a part of the flames
and can be certain this is death's failure and life's victory.
When we wake,
we are not a person,
those who wear short trousers,
those who wear mid-length trousers,
those who wear long trousers, [1]
those who walk mountain path and lose their balance
the high-pitched voice of the soul.
Oh, mountains of the world,
heroic ornaments on the mountains' navel,
whether you are armor for a man or a woman,
everyone who sees you
will stand on the flames
and spin in dance for the highest honor,
the sacrificed ox-head is covered
with scribbled stars and the moon,
this is primeval sharing,
the opposite of a theoretical Utopia,
they sit on the slopes of the earth
receiving their hosts' food,
and here we can trust

all the lips that pass the cup of liquor
will become one clan's
gigantic bowl floating on the horizon.
Oh, the horse race of humankind,
who established the only rule,
that the legendary horse Dali'azong will never die,
because each day his name is spoken.
In the ring, they turn the riders
into abstract concepts and nothingness,
only the winners can become
a kernel in an arcing gaze,
true beauty cannot be reproduced,
selecting a Ganmoa Girl for this era,
hidden between agate and silver,
we once sacrificed our lives for beauty.
An unnamed singer
cries out from a burning throat,
paying tribute to freedom, paying tribute to the flames,
paying tribute to forgetting, paying tribute to memory,
and we in this earth's cockfight,
the mestizos in Mexico's cockfight
their mouths open in a smile on our faces,
and we hail them
in the shadow of their fighting roosters
like a bundle of flames without foreheads.
Oh, our mountains,
our yesterday, today, and perhaps tomorrow
will meet you amid the clear reality
in a mysterious inner world,
and because of your existence,
every poet and singer here
will offer you all that involves you
from their own lives,
along with happiness, sadness, tears,
and the last soliloquy slipping back into the flames.

Translated by Eleanor Goodman

Zizipuwu[1]

Place where the ancestors' spirits gather.
    White spreads
across the entire territory, and there is no
    concept of time,
weightless beings stroll here, children and
    the elderly
beyond life and death, their youth and age

rejecting existential changes by another means.
The constellations are within reach, the phantoms of birds
sink into the great sea of light. The spirit horse with his drooping
    golden wings
stands on the other shore of perception, and everything is newly
    defined.
The sun's countenance solidifies into a tranquil white screen,
while chanted texts flow through the soundless enormous source.

Arriving from different directions, voices of the led
are summoned on the path. The flames' eulogy
is a gift from the high priest to the three spirits, its accompaniment
stays far from demon world dangers. White wool held in the hand,
both hands carrying grapes grown fat from spring water. Do not
    hesitate.
This is not a place to remain, the classics record
all cities turn to dust in the end, and for the part that remains
destruction is indisputable. Immaterial
entities wallow forever in immortality,
otherwise they couldn't give significance to all that is temporary.

There is no god of time, and if there is still
this sort of time, its back will not be
covered in the firmament's nails. Oh, the only honor
is souvenirs that bloom in life and are collectively owned.

---

[1] Zizipuwu is the sacred place to which the souls of the Yi people return. It is located in the hinterland of the Zhaotong Plateau in Yunnan, across the Jinsha River from Sichuan.

Infuse epics with oxblood, heroes memorialized by the generations,
the saddle on the wall searching for its rider.
Opportunity for revelry, with splendor revolving around bodies,
forgetting silver-bedecked masks during the festival of fire.
This is the contract between the body and the soul, their fight
will represent the hidden secrets at the beginning of life and death.

Oh, poet, great high priest! This is
the reason we chant before crowds.
Forgive me, there was a brief moment
I was corrupted by passion's demands, and forgot to recite
the pearl-like verses. But when the flames once again
illuminate the path before mankind, you will still
see me standing in the front ranks of the ancient clans.
In the traditional ceremony, eternal life does not choose
an exterior shape, and although the forehead's changes from age
are unstoppable, imagination makes me yearn to cry out:
lamenting that little birds can no longer arc above the earthen wall.

Flames change the body's form more than anything else,
they take existing things up to a metaphysical nation.
Dress the dead in clothes that will never rot,
and only with that power can they reach that unknown territory.
Never believe that life and death have been explained by clever
    people,
otherwise, the abstract 'one' would unfold into the infinite,
a conclusion said to have been discovered by a madman.
Let everything wrapped in fire never have so-called weight again,
life must have a day when it becomes free and easy.

There is only the recurring process of birth and death,
the oxhorn trumpet blows traces of blood that wrap around the
    bobbin.
The long wait makes angry reproduction cry out,
and turns uncivilized lovers into tormenting adversaries,
when a vision of gold branches cuts open the assembly in the
    moonlight,

this is called a carnival of the eyes, finally welcoming
the convulsive return and release of the image beneath the flesh.
There, red cloth winds around the acclaim of the victors,
there, maternal vibrations draw in the cycles.

The liberated spirit crosses the door of the constellations,
music announces the stairs of dawn amid the mountains' daytime.
All spirits will forget the happiness of the senses,
solemn as a metaphor for the opposite of a piece of black iron.
Quickly play the four mouth-harps' irrational masterpiece,
there the white sheep and transparent birds
will receive the gods' well-deserved praise.
We should clap when faced with the free liberation of a soul,
welcoming their loved ones to stand solemnly in Zizipuwu.

Translated by Eleanor Goodman

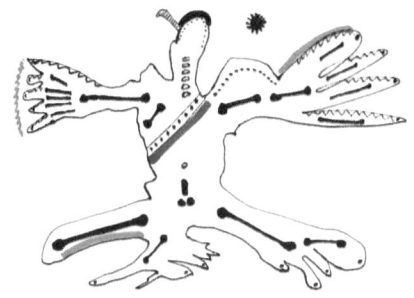

神鹰之子　2017.2.15　JDMj 梦皆画州

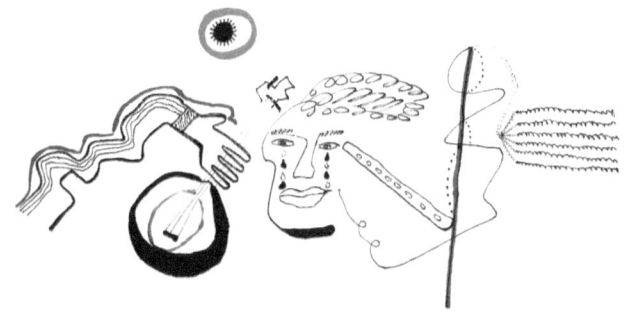

月琴与笛子　2017.2.15　JDMj 梦皆画州

西界的声音　2017.2.15　JDMj 梦皆画州

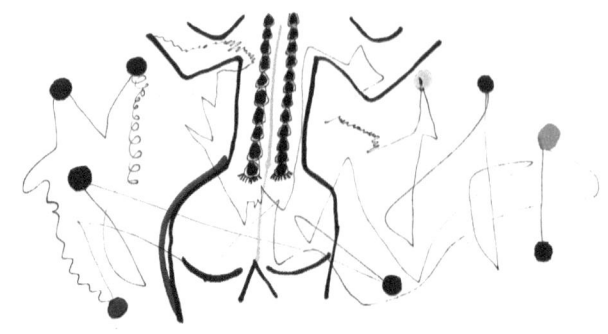

黑色加辫子　　2017.2.25 JDMj

穿裹装的妈。2017.2.16 JDMj

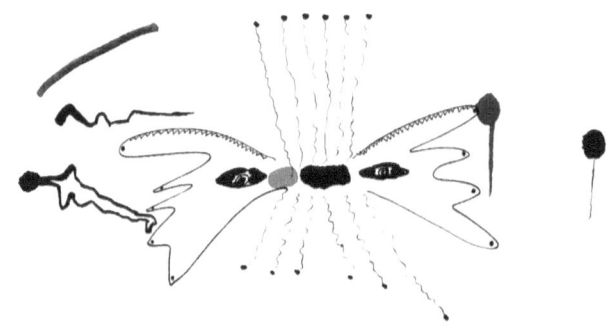

无题之二　2017.2.15 JDMj

禹語者　2017.2.15 JDMj

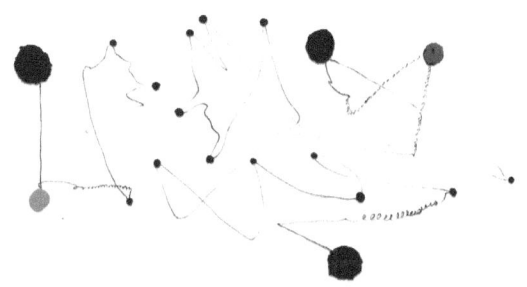
北年記物預言　2017.2.15 JDMj

8禹0和姐妹伯　2017.2.16 JDMj

不死的三魂　2017.2.15　JDMj　曾强田小川

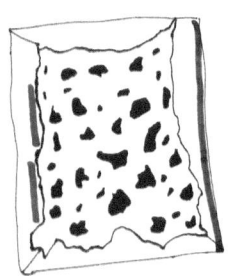

牛皮上記憶的殘片　JDMj　曾强田小川 2017.2.15

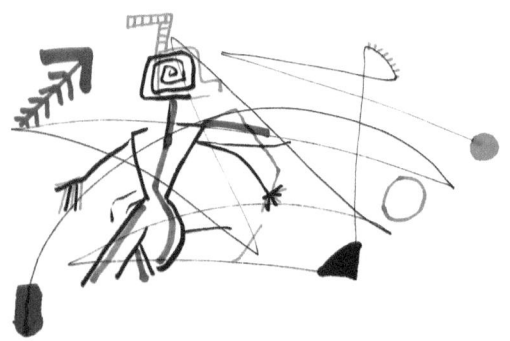

神靈的力量　2017.2.15　JDMj　曾强田小川

穿盛装的勇士　2017.2.15 JDMj 哥哥回忆

背皮画的人　2017.2.15 JDMj 哥哥回忆

我的父亲　2017.2.15 JDMj 哥哥回忆

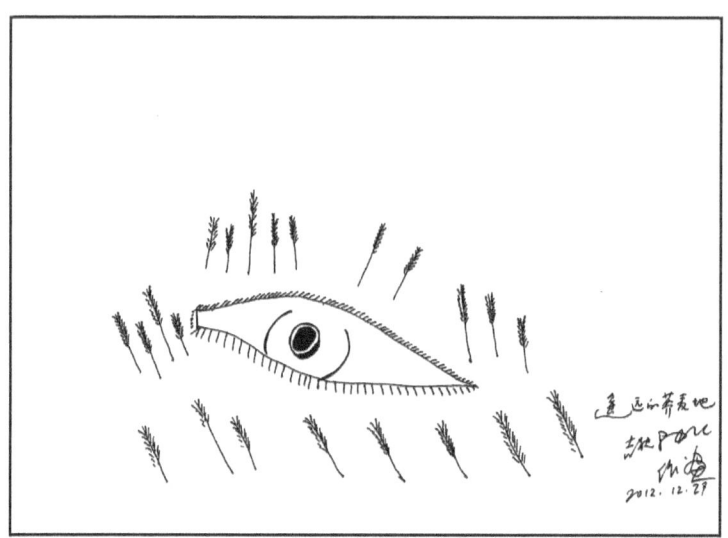

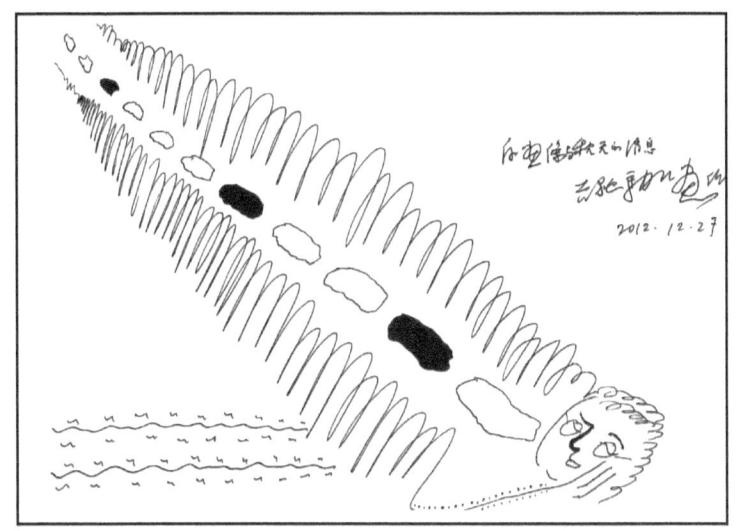

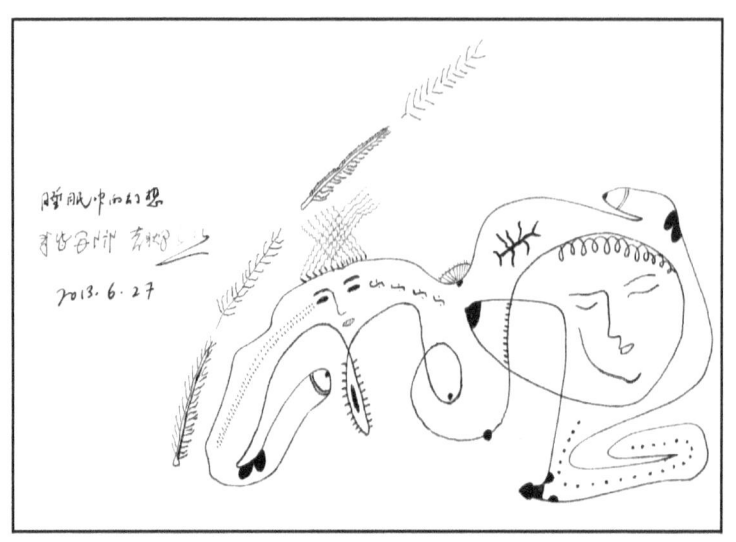

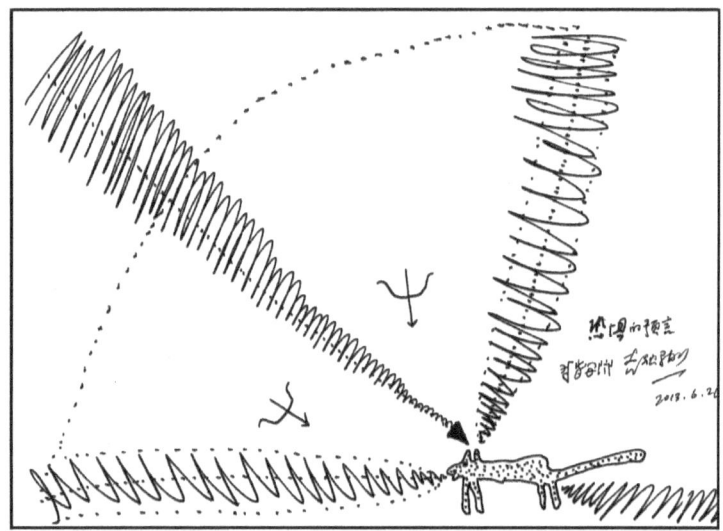

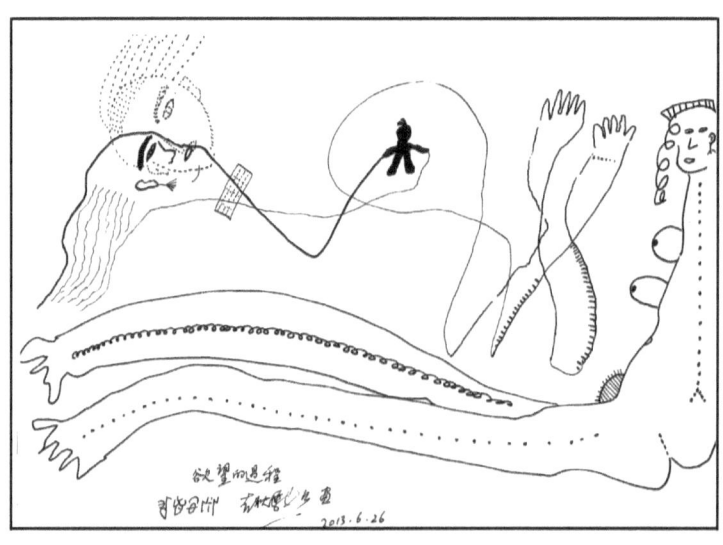

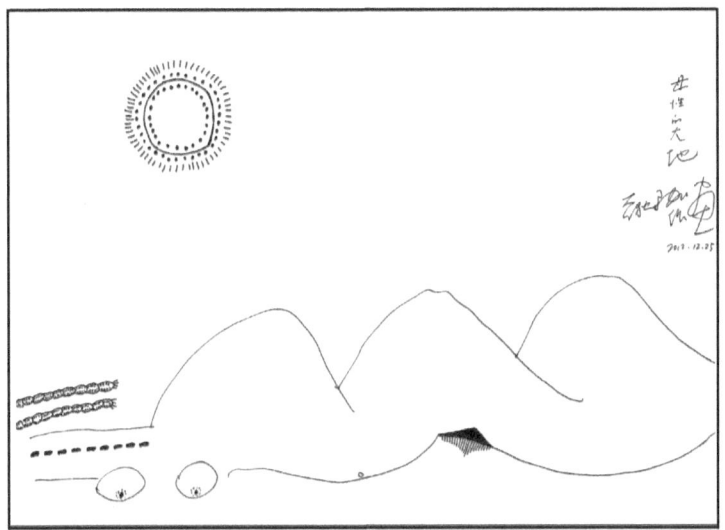

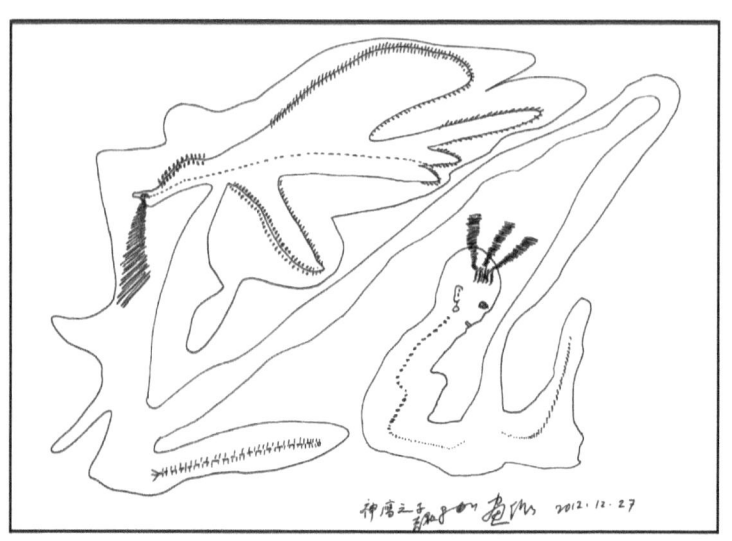

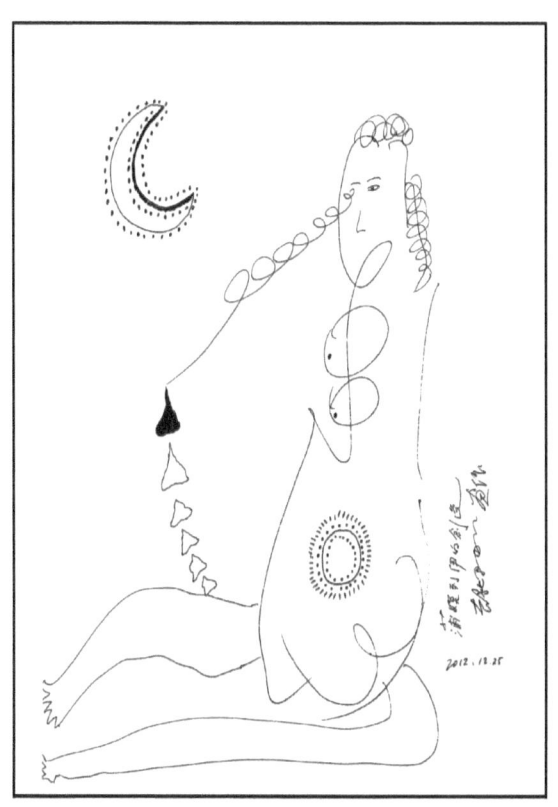

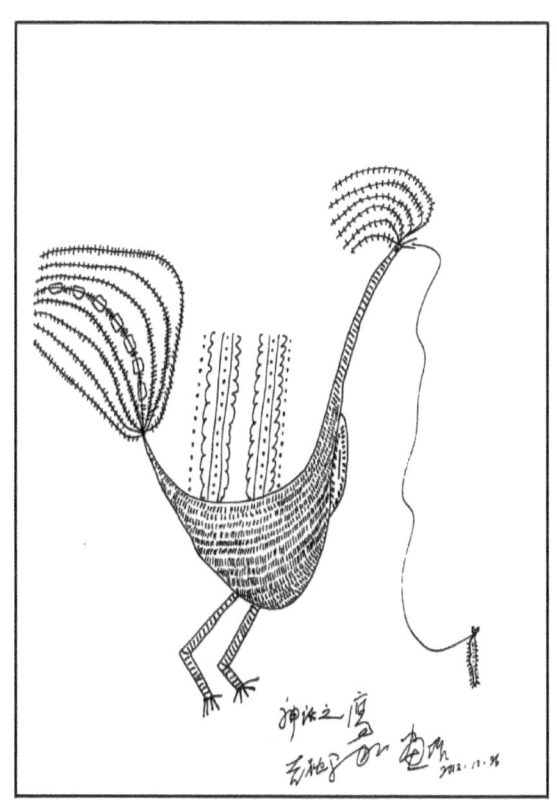

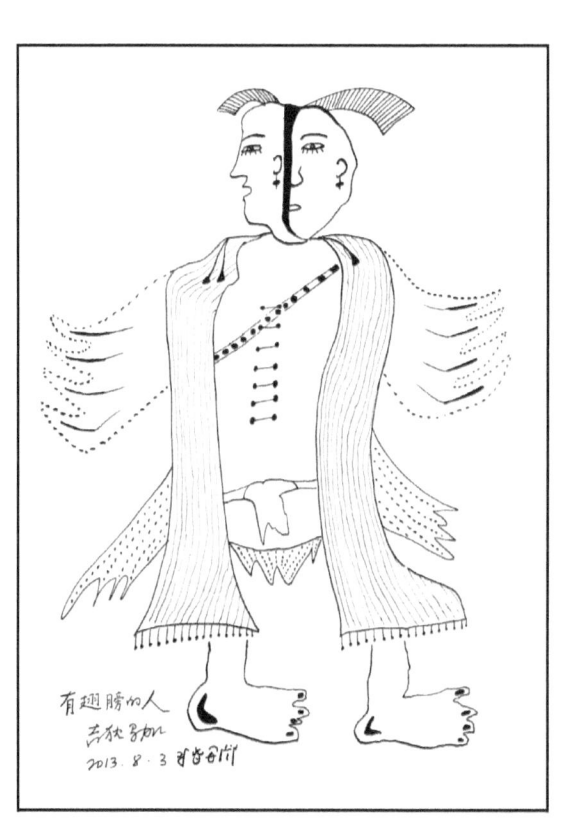

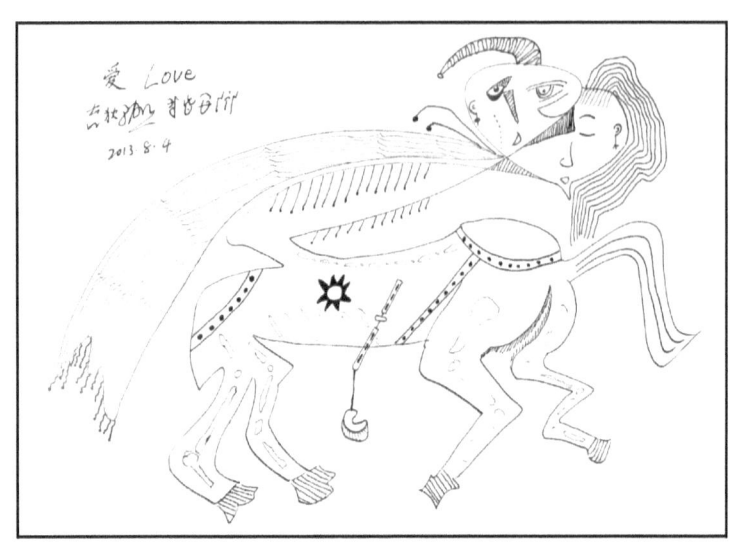

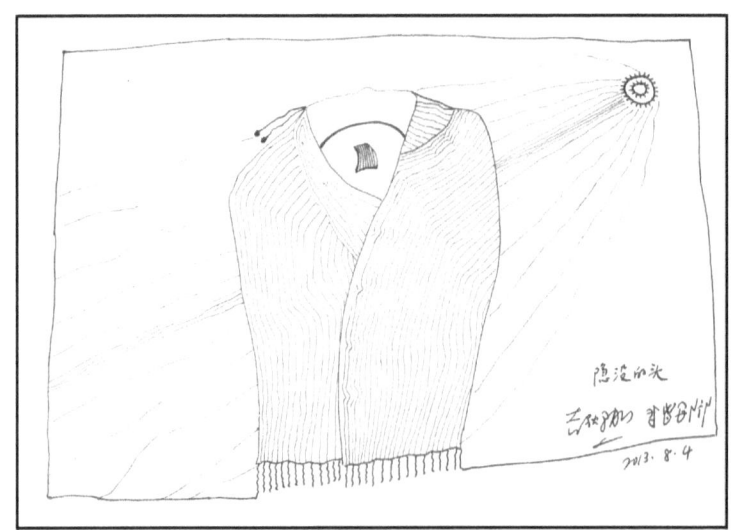

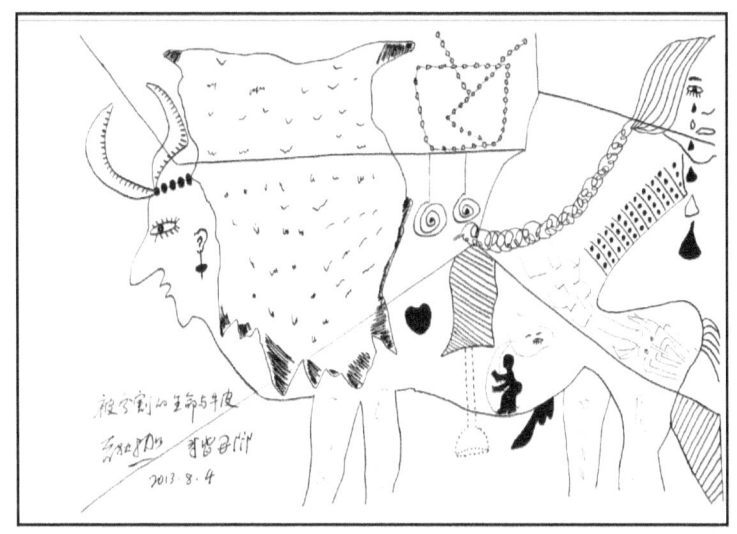
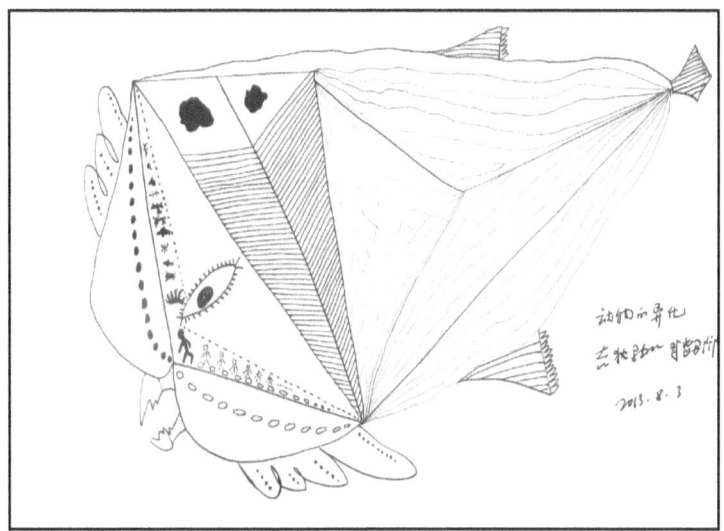

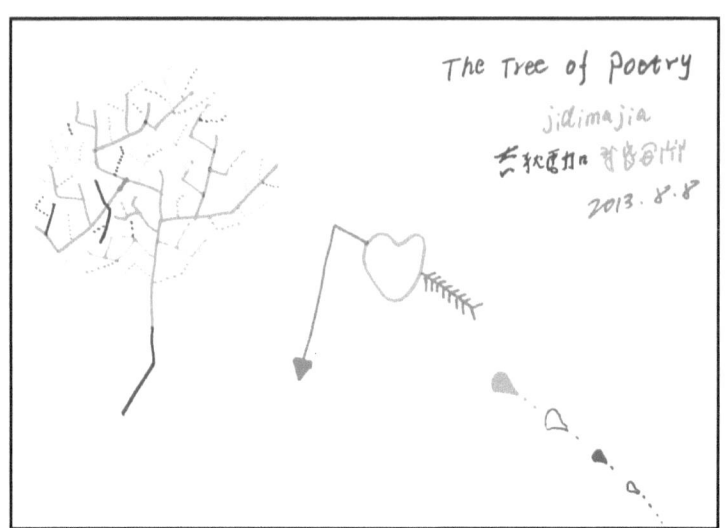
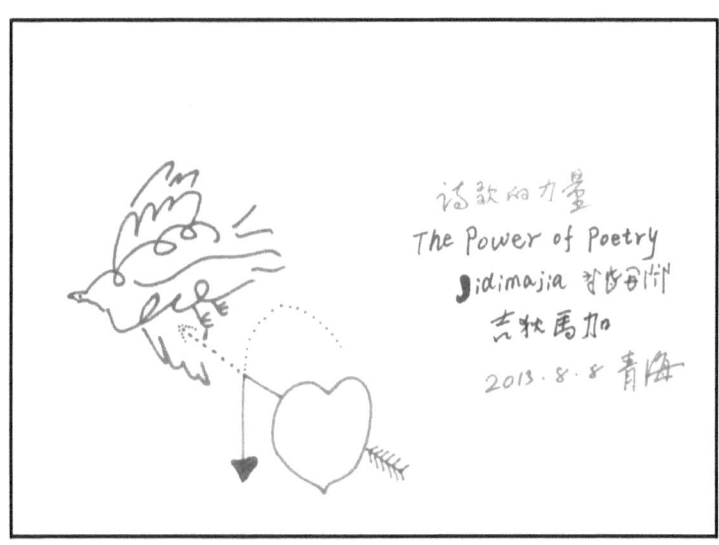

Literary lectures and interviews

Du Fu's Thatched Cottage—Both a Reality and a Legend

—Address at the Opening Ceremony of 2017 International Festival of Poetry & Liquor

Be it in China or any other country in the world, there are certain haunts of the great writers and poets who have worked and lived being immortalized and sanctified to posterity. No other place like the present hamlet (expanded now into a huge park) holds such a special place in the hearts of the Chinese nation and Chinese poets.

This cottage has been so extensively commemorated and celebrated by posterity, in so many novels, poems, anecdotes, and legends in the past millennium that it has become an abstraction instead of a reality, an arch icon of the golden age of the Chinese Tang poetry, the apogee of one of the most important poetic schools of the Classic Chinese poetry in general.

It should be emphasized that our Poet Saint, after whose name this cottage has been named, represents a great tradition, the tradition of Confucianism, which is the state religion and state ideology for the Chinese mind since the Han dynasty, is one of the three greatest spiritual pillars of the medieval and contemporary civilized world. As Jesus speaks of love, Buddha, of compassion, Confucius makes the core mental paraphernalia of the elite, the scholar, mandarin, poet, the twin preoccupation with the wellbeing of the common people who struggle and crave for happiness and the political fate of the nation. Because of this, Du Fu's poems have been epic-class testament to the turbulence and violence of the Mid Tang and immensity of the sufferings sustained by the civil society in depth and artistry unrivalled by any of his contemporaries.

Du Fu is not only Poet Saint for China, but also compares supremely with any other great poet in his time and of all time. Kenneth Rexroth says he has saturated himself with Du Fu's poetry for forty-five years and confesses Du Fu has made him "a better man, as a moral agent and a perceiving organism."

Du Fu's prime years overlapped with the worst years of the Tang. Yet the personal misfortune proved to be the fortune of the Chinese poetry in its classic phase. Due to the collapse of central authority and the subsequent famine, devastations, Du Fu spent his mature years in wandering, retreat or exile. As the most famous tenant of Chengdu and Shu of all time, he wrote a number of poems now being masterpieces chanted by primary school goers and established poets alike. For depth of observation of the political chaos of his time, and craftsmanship, for praise of love, magnanimity, calm and compassion, his recipe to redeem the nightbound world, Du Fu is unsurpassed and unprecedented.

Both a legend and a reality, this cottage has been the Mecca of Chinese poets over centuries. Du Fu sang up unabashedly Shu land's landscape and natural bounty, not without a reason. The agricultural potential and the strategic position elevated it to a major Chinese granary, commercial and cultural center since the Han and Tang which spawned an aura, imperceptibly and unobtrusively, to nurture the growth of Chinese poetry rarely seen anywhere in China or in the world.

An overview of Chinese history of literature will lead us to a discovery that Shu land (contemporary Sichuan) has always been associated with many a great poet and artist in ancient China. It has been argued that the finest flower of Chinese culture is poetry and poetry has certainly embodied the spiritual dimension of the Chinese people supposedly without a religion as center of spirit.

The successful inauguration of this poetry festival affords us solace and assurance that so many great poets from all corners of the globe are gathered in this cottage, consecrated and dedicated to Du Fu, in defense of the sanctity of poetry and the hallowing of one of the greatest poet saints China has to offer to the world. Momentarily we all revert to another time, another place and we are all Du Fu's contemporaries. This cottage, unfazed by any storm, unshaken by any wind, has been deeply enshrined in the inner recesses of the human psyche in their quest for justice and freedom in defiance of all the evil and dark forces, as malicious and sinister in Du Fu's time as in ours.

Because of this, I am fully convinced, hoisting the torch of poetry in our hands, as long as human eyes can see, men can breathe, poetry will outlast and human songs will forever prevail upon the face of our troubled planet.

Translated by Huang Shaozheng

A City Hemmed in with Radiant Beams of Poetry
—Address at the Opening Ceremony of 2017 Chengdu International Poetry Week

This ancient city, Chengdu, under discussion, with no aesthetic appeal in its modern contours notwithstanding, is very special in the sense of being both sublunary and fairy, locus of sensibility and spirit, taking wings to the skies instantly by alchemies of imagination, when we attempt to associate things urban with the poetic side of human beings, especially to probe into the fortuitous converging of its physical topography and metaphoric coordinates. A widely travelled man, I have roamed among the many charming cities of many countries on the planet; if I am approached with similar questions like "which city do you believe is mostly akin in ethos, in aura of enchantment to poetry?" my answer out of hand would be Chengdu in China and Paris of France. Some, I am aware, might not agree to my pride and prejudice, as there is no accounting for taste.

It is greatly to be debated on my part that both Chengdu and Paris seem to be possessed with some inner ethos or mystery of sensibility qualified to be called capitals of poetry, not only because Chengdu has, over centuries, produced, and been home to a dozen of great poets, also because many major artistic movements that have impinged substantially upon literary histories of both China and the world. The near-cult status accorded to poetry has justifiably lulled Chinese into believing Chengdu is a city famed for the depth and sophistication of its poetic heritage.

Paris, of course, has its own share of laureates. What has perennially intrigued me is that Chengdu has continually and continuously radiated a nationwide image of inexhaustible poetic creativity, flaunting an envious continuity of tradition even since the city was born 4th century BC. While Tang dynasty, the golden of the most golden ages for Chinese poetry, saw an extraordinary efflorescence of poetic blossoms, Chengdu has unbelievably never been short of good poets who have chronicled the China experience, the mutations of the human condition, joie de vivre or the human idiocies of this world. Indeed Chengdu has beckoned to an awesome array of genius. Li Bai, Du Fu, Bai Juyi, Cen Shen, Liu Yuxi, Gao Shi, Yuan Zhen, Jia Dao, Li Shangyin, Wen Tingyun, and not to mention the four talents of the early Tang, many of whom had sojourned here. Du Fu, our Poet Saint, loyal repeat visitor, made Chengdu as his home and lingered in retreat for three years and nine months, leaving a legacy of 200 poems extolling the virtues of common folks here and around.

In a sense, Chengdu has been the spiritual home of poets wandering or in exile. *Hark to the Poet Immortal* when Li Bai sang up:

From nine celestial vaunts emerges Chengdu
Where towns and villages loom like scrolls
Grass, trees, clouds and mountains all as chic as brocade
Whose beauty beyond compare anything China proper offers.

What Li Bai so evocatively sums up does not strike only a personal note, as he is, among others, more appreciative of the subtleties and richness of culture and nature of Chengdu both as resident and poet.

Equally worthy of note is the first anthology of *Ci Poems* ever to be published in Chengdu which dates at 941, compiled by scholar official Zhao Chongzuo, inclusive of five hundred Ci poems, authored by poets, many being non-natives, spanning over one century long, foretelling the dawn of a larger renaissance in days to come. We are talking about another peak performance of Chinese lyrical poets in the Song dynasty in the brewing. The anthology turns out to be a major cataclysm in triggering the greatest outpourings of lyricism sweeping Song times.

In a way, Chengdu has been historically turbulent, surviving devastations of many a renegade independent state and runaway kingdom skirmishing with another or defying central authority. "Order and peace breaks down first in Shu and restores the last in the country", so the ancients aptly put it. Yet, in all fairness, for much of its eventful history, Chengdu reveled in its prosperity, grateful for the strategic geography and cultural splendor which had elevated it to one of the commercial and cultural centers in medieval and contemporary China alike. Agricultural innovations, the installation of the Dujiang Yan Irrigation System, in particular, opened up Chengdu Plain to intensive farming, which quickly transformed the area into an economic base, a cornerstone of Chinese society. Thanks to this and others, Chengdu leapt to periodic prominence at several major national crises.

Where nowadays tourists predominate, Chengdu has always been rendevousing with artists and poets as it has been celebrated in so many poems, stories, anecdotes, paintings for one important reason: remoteness from the whirlwinds of Chinese politics in Central Plains and the famed nonchalance of local population who are nicely laid back, reclining on bamboo couches, idling away all day long, indulgent in their staid teahouse culture and gentle pace of living. Such perfect location and slowing down of life provide the best sanctuary for many wandering and troubled souls looking for a temporary relief. I am not idealizing the lives of struggling poor artists and nobility of peasantry. I am merely reminding you at certain historical moments, Sichuan was the place for some poets fleeing wars and other disasters, and indeed, for centuries past, feudal, agrarian, Sichuan has been much sustained and contained within a considerable measure of self sufficiency in terms of produce and supply of food, cotton, cloth, copper, iron, salt, fur, tea and wine—all being prerequisites for bare subsistence of lower caste and the elite in their attempt to create the good life.

Of course, such self-sufficiency bred naturally a bias of outlook and petty-minded Philistinism. For one thing, local budding talents, as a rule, don't get scouted and recognized unless they move on beyond the secluded territory. This is, of course, not to deny Sichuan is a source for great men. Li Bai in the Tang dynasty, the Three Sus of the Song dynasty, are four of the most illustrious poets on hand. In contemporary China, lots of giants, such as poet Guo Moruo, novelists Ba Jin and Li Jieren, master painter Zhang Daqian, short story writers Sha Ting and Ai Wu have illuminated the night of Chinese culture and the list of artists and poets can go on without end. Reaffirming the global weight of Sichuan, one must mention the name of Deng Xiaoping, who having initiated the late 1970s' reform and opening up to the world, the classic way to guarantee distinction and eminence if followed assiduously, has once for all put China on the map of one of the foremost places among the relatively well to do, advanced civilizations of the world, say, in a brief space of three decades. The rise of these great minds and the vital roles they have played all take us back to the beginnings of greatness, that is, they were all born here, got educated or spent a certain portion of their memorable adolescence or youth in this beloved city of ours.

We are rightly proud of Chengdu as our native Guo Moruo's launching pad to blaze the path of New Poetry a hundred years ago. In 1910, Guo first landed in Chengdu, Study in Sichuan Higher Learning Institute and groomed himself as the future standard bearer of New Poetry. Novelist Li Jieren's lifelong passions and theme are this land that has endowed him with a pathos and lyricism that earns him the renown of master of regionalism, on a par with Lao She. Great humanitarian writer Ba Jin came from a family of officials and scholars, residing in the grand Li Mansion in Zhengtongshun Street and rose to fame by his trilogy of *Family, Spring* and *Autumn*, half autobiography, half revelation, all being classic tales of social oppression despairing of a past beyond redemption and dreaming of a tantalizing future out of reach. For a blistering look at the decadent society, Ba Jin offers the remedy of compassion, love and magnanimity.

Master Painter Zhang Daqian, fleeing war torn interior China, settled down in Chengdu in 1938 to complete his masterpieces *Mountains in Shu* and *Rivers of Shu*. In reaffirmation of traditional landscape techniques, Zhang expanded and finally exploded into dynamic fury, ink, movement, color, line—that are ingeniously patterned but in such cluttered abundance as to appear unprecedented—almost, by hindsight, tantamount to a revolution in spearheading Chinese painting in sync with post-impressionist trends in France. Zhang's artistic activity in Chengdu attests ultimately to his genius in pacesetting Chinese expression of artistic styles in modern times.

When I speak of Chengdu and Paris have same breath, they both to me demonstrate a continuity of tradition while evincing an ability to learn and absorb things foreign and new to a preeminent degree, an aura enticing and luring poets and artists with alien cultural background to make Chengdu their comfort zone. Some cultural critics and sociologists postulate, not without good reasons, that some city was conceived and built for poets, thinkers and artists.

For those familiar with Chinese poetry, an overview of what happened culturally in the late 1970s and the early 1980s when Chinese poetry, deriving inspiration from French or Anglophone or Spanish models, began to free itself from the orthodox rigidity of Soviet realism, whose far-reaching and profound repercussions are still felt today, will lead one to one bold claim Chengdu has staked out: as an alternate center of stylistic innovation together with Beijing perhaps in complementary pairs, like Li Bai and Du Fu, a phenomenon deserving pondering as it must represent some historic need to keep human faculties in balance. Hence the legend due to two essential facts, (i.e., Chengdu's poets population growing ever beyond count and the poetic schools mushrooming to such unfettered scale), as to concretize and corroborate this city's power and status, if not greater than that of Beijing. It is not boastful at all to say over two dozen of established contemporary Chinese poets, still clinging to the honored career with gusto and vitality, are Chengdunese, former residents or still natives. Claim is here equal to boast: Chengdu, besides Beijing, defines Chinese poetry and possesses an ingrained lineage, without peer by any other city in China. It is the country's artistic bank together with Beijing.

So to speak, the city of Chengdu retains pockets of Tang and Song's elegant spiritual past, an inheritance of certain traits atypical, some marks very stubborn to be erased in the inner layers of the collective psyche of a race, a group, carried over from generation to generation. And in the last analysis, is there any city under the sun that does not have cultural genes of its own to be inherited in a linear progression? My answers are of course, in the affirmative definitely. Although Chengdu is a city in flux culturally and socially, it still lures poets from all directions for the same compelling reason: the visiting of so many haunts of so many native great poets and artists who have lived, worked and played here. The idea alone will send a vicarious thrill down your literary spine as you will discover the city's genuine splendor and firm link with budding and maturing years of so many wonderful artists and poets, especially the presence of mementos of Li Bai and Du Fu, two minds conterminous in their depth and scope with the poetic limits of man. The fact that 2017 Chengdu International Poetry Week is inaugurated today in honor of Chengdu's glorious past, as reflected in its rich legacy of art and poetry, evidenced by the attendance of so many distinguished poets home and abroad, has proved the fullness of the truth value of my point.

Fellow poets and friends, don't you see, right in front of you, under your very noses, a city hemmed in with radiant beams of poetry?

Translated by Huang Shaozheng

Heavenly Stones Made of Eagle Wings and Light
—Remarks at the Opening Ceremony of the 2nd Liangshan, Xichang Silk Road International Poetry Week

It is my pleasure to welcome you, on behalf of the organizing committee, in my capacity as both deputy chairman of China Writers Association and chairman of the organizing committee, to the 2nd Liangshan, Xichang Silk Road International Poetry Week on the occasion of this grand opening ceremony. I, for one, wish for a most successful operation of the week. My heartfelt gratitude must be also registered here for the wonderful myriad preparatory work put in by all individuals, institutions and the organizing staff to make this event a reality.

Friends, our world is a world characterized by turmoil and uncertainty. How we humans, inhabiting different quarters of this world, choose the life we lead in the forthcoming future is the common challenge before us all. Other than on the political planes whereupon politicians wrack their brains to come out with schemes and programs as how to construct a new world order amenable to justice, peace and sustainable development, we need also draw in the wisdom and insight from other sectors of the society to better cope with the crisis lurking ahead and co-develop while seeking common ground on major issues and reserving differences on minor ones.

The One Belt, One Road Initiative, proposed by Chinese President Xi Jinping is a most visionary blueprint to maneuver, hitch and move our world towards the direction with a shared future, woe or joy, rain or sunshine. Because of this, dialogues and interactions involving various cultures, races and religions have the potential to iron out the differences and oil the wheels of history. Poetry, as the best flower of each culture, more than any other social or political parameters, stands to create a status quo out of a plethora of problems, either racial or religious or cultural in origin. Poetry has the unique power to alleviate mistrust and generate a feeling of brotherhood and fraternity where only hate and injustice existed before.

Friends, the above lapse conjures up a sophisticated metaphor of "heavenly stones upon eagle wings and light" in my mind. Look, the ageless sun has never failed, on its chariot across the immense vaults of the sky to perform its daily patrol over this Yi region of ranged mountains, silent and speechless from the primordial times, flora and fauna, life forms bustling and hustling making their homely rounds. Likewise, light and shadow of time have never ceased flickering upon the sublunary world of light and darkness. Only if you are convinced of the ultimate fact of all living things being not isolated atomic substances and issuing from one common hidden source, your heart and soul can merge with the reality before your eyes that is in no way virtual and fairy.

What do we make of this occultist revelation? Well, personally I am unswervingly of the opinion that even a grain of dust acts and is acted upon as part of the overarching cosmos. The idea is, tiny and infinitesimal a grain of dust might be, it is nevertheless, self-sufficient, a cosmos carrying its own share of energy and information, defying any reductionist attempt in the positivistic vein.

Left alone to a quiet corner of this vast domain of ours, I sometimes pause and take stock, my eyes shut and my ears open, to hear a distinct, though somewhat obliterated, soliloquy of wind in praise of light coming from the depths of time, the incarnation of truth we are on the threshold of witnessing. No wonder the great German poet

Holderlin, in his poems, always identifies the supernatural as heralding the creation of a sacred spiritual language worthy of poetry. He is best read as a poet divinely inspired.

Yi is such a people of history, culture and tradition that as one of the 9 million descendants, I am rightly proud of the oceanic repository of historic texts, mostly epics, left to us by our ancestors and I fully embrace our forefathers recalcitrant and relentless cosmological penchant, among other things, our deeply felt interrelatedness of humans with all creatures as well as our due respect for the law of impermanence of life and death as a precondition of mortal existence. As a poet inheriting such grand intangible matrimony, a sense of pride and being fully blessed swells up that I feel entitled to enhance my Yi heritage by initiating a process of renaissance, revitalization and regeneration worthy of the Yi spirituality.

Legacies do not just happen and persist. To be meaningful, we must keep negotiating between them and our contemporary life and carry on with the great task our ancestors have so nobly pioneered and advanced. For a people famed for hero worship, we draw inexhaustible inspiration from our animistic faith and tradition made up of an unrivalled wealth of creation epics such as: *Hnewo Teyy, Asei-po Seiji, Amo Xinimo, Chamu, Meige, Shamanic Scripture of the Lolos, On the Cosmos and Human Learning, Origins of the Yi People, The All-Engulfing Flood*, all being now common assets of mankind, commending themselves despite adulators or debunkers. Yet, this is no time for wistful thinking or nostalgic retreat. Culture changes, shifts and perishes if it does not adapt with time. This is the moment to recharge ourselves and set off on a new mission to be undertaken by our generation, that is, to actually quarry new sky stones, worthy of Yi legend, fit for the vaults of heaven.

Of course, poets from across the world are all born with the mandate to create their own heavenly stones upon eagle wings and light. Under our pens should flow poems that reach into the hearts of our people and make them laugh, cry, feel and think. Our voices should be raised anew in celebration of human glory and toil, our passionate search for justice, our tender loves and profoundest longings.

Dear friends, let's ignite our torches to light our way, convinced of the invincible justice prevailing upon a globe "with limping sway disabled" eventually, loyal perennially to the dual principles of sanctity and freedom of each individual simply because the heavenly stones so much treasured are out there for us to be hit upon and quarried. Let this be realized among men that our footsteps forward will not be halted and reversed on our way towards a promising tomorrow. Thank you.

Translated by Huang Shaozheng

Poets Are Still the Moral Leaders of the Civic Society Today
—Written replies to Graham Mort

Graham Mort: What is a poem for? How do you see its function in relation to human culture historically and in the future?

Jidi Majia: Poetry is as old as human history, the primary mode of human spiritual life as the identity of a poet in primitive religions strides the offices of tribal chiefs and shamans, and in most ancient societies poetry bridges man and heaven & earth and communions man with supernatural beings. In essence, poetry is the purest human creation, not only linguistically a magical sublimation but also indispensable in the human spirit to create hallucinogens, that is to say, as long as human spiritual needs dictate, poetry will survive. And it's not going to die, that's what I believe. Either from the perspective of reality and the future based on the particularity of poetry, poetry is a remarkable part of human culture. Of course, as culture varies from time to time, there will be changes, but there will always be portions of it stabilized and fixed, becoming what we call by the name of tradition or canon. Such is the interaction of reality and poetry and the constancy of which explains the marginality of poetry in this present era of consumerism and rampant materialism. But it also tells us poetry does have an irreplaceable role in the spiritual life and cultural continuity of mankind. If it is believed that the spiritual life is an absolute necessity for mankind, then poets and poetry will continue to be with us, although that does not preclude the further worsening of the fate of poets.

Graham Mort: How do you see the relationship between the forms of written text and the sounds and music of poetry?

Jidi Majia: In a way poetry is a kind of form, a form of linguistic construct. Since the importance of writing and textuality is self-evident, in many cases textual innovation and even poetic innovation are equally important, so much so they do have much in common with innovations that have occurred to painting and music, either in synchronic or diachronic terms. We all agree what holds true, I mean, the tenets of painting of Pericles' Greece does not for Renaissance painters and the successive emergence of practitioners of impressionism, fauvism, cubism, futurism commonly dubbed modern art falsify those of Classical Greece or 18th century French tradition. The same is true with poetry, I mean the absolute need for innovation for both visual art and poetry. As poetry is written, it means one thing for sure, that poetic innovation is essentially linguistic reshaping of the status of poetry, and for poetry its inner form like tone and rhythm or prosody is thrust into eternal alteration to the extent we might say this constitutes the life of poetry. If the prosodic side of poetry stagnates, then the inner life of poetry ceases. Indeed, tone and rhythm are the hearts of poetry, or metaphorically the roar of blood vessels of poetry. That partially accounts for the notorious complaint of the impossibility of poetic translation. I reckon the content, or the sense to be made, the message to be imparted is only partial trouble. The sound, the prosodic aspect of poetry, the tone and rhythm prove more troublesome. Great poets are great because they are good at identifying and catching the poetic voice of each nation. Invariably they are also deemed the voice of their own people.

Graham Mort: How can the mythological dimensions of poetry be reconciled with contemporary scientific knowledge?

Jidi Majia: No poet's writing is breaking away from tradition, and many poets even if they are stranded and caught in the rather complex realities and intricacies of history of each nation, they are not quarantined from their own tradition and history. One obvious evidence is the rewriting myth repeatedly among poets in different eras. Modern Greek poet George Seferis's masterpiece *Myth-History*, his compatriot Odysseas Elytis's epic *The Axion Esti* are both written to treat Greek myth with a modern sensibility, both being finest specimen of building up the mythology and institutions of today's Hellenism since both poets won the Nobel Prize in Literature. They compose poems to rid their countrymen's conscience from remorses unjustifiable, to achieve the highest degree of lucidity in expression, to find true solace in their cultural heritage and to finally succeed in approaching the mystery of light. Another great Greek poet, Nikos Kazantzakis, published his monumental poem *The Odyssey: A Modern Sequel* in 1960, an epic of 33,000 verses in which he praises in behalf of modern man in the prototype of Odyssey the passionate though tragic search for freedom as well as paints an image of ordinary people engaged in the incessant strife between spirit and flesh, their redemption and resurrection. In all these giants mentioned above, we can see the mythical element reconciled with modern scientific knowledge and their relationship is by no means an antagonistic one. On the contrary, they all succeed in merging a modern sensibility with a historical perspective which is a fundamental problem bedeviling all ancient civilizations in modern times.

Graham Mort: How might new information and communications technology affect poetic form and publication in the future?

Jidi Majia: We are living in an era of globalization and the internet which in fact offers new possibilities for the spread of poetry, and even robots are said to be capable of composing poems, no? I'm not worried about poetry being written and spread in new channels and tools. What I am really worried about is the possible scenario of all poets becoming robot-like, parroting and copying one another, with no individuality or personality; then what is the rason d'etre for poets to go on writing and living in the name of poetry? For sure one thing we need not worry about is that robots may one day overrun us technically and rhetorically, but they certainly will not be able to win the hearts and souls, for as long as human poetry exists in the hearts and minds, robots without souls cannot defeat us. Now, thousands of poems are being churned out every day on the internet, and their spread may take some of the most exotic forms and speed. Unprecedented? Yes. But still, this is not the end of the world. We simply must muster up courage and intellect enough to take the measure of it and make the true sense of it.

Graham Mort: In a globalized world with interlocking political and economic structures what is the poet's role as social commentator and moral leader?

Jidi Majia: The reality of globalization, as well as the attendant transformations so triggered and caused, should predispose poets to be engaged, aesthetically and socially since the fact of so many people consumed by rampant consumerism and crass materialism should serve as a clarion call to all poets to action. To say poets should be the conscience of our age does not mean we should sit in judgment on the world but in that he should uphold a torch, a candle as illuminator: he is a participant, a witness, a critic of the age he is living in. I am aware I am echoing Shelley's central faith in poets being the ultimate upholder and preserver of great virtues that distinguish man from all other species on earth.

Graham Mort: How can poetry mediate between minority ethnic groups and more dominant groupings within societies?

Jidi Majia: A poet's relationship with the outside world is both simple and complex. It depends. Ideally, poetry should be at the center of various ethnic and social class relations, binding them and mediating in case there is dispute, a view held by Irish poets Yeats and Heaney, especially the latter one whose writings suggest the poet as healer of ancient wounds and feuds that divide British–Irish peoples. They also deem themselves as custodians and defenders of Irish culture and tradition, more importantly as those of the spirit of human freedom. Indeed, great poetry must transcend all insularity of ideology and partisanship of ism and act as repository of common property of universal human significance. A true poet must also hold high the banner of friendship, peace and humanity to truly promote harmonious coexistence and friendly exchanges among different races and nations.

Graham Mort: How important is it that poets communicate internationally and how might such links develop the poem as an inter-cultural phenomenon?

Jidi Majia: Poetic communication between different countries and across different cultural background barriers is always a bonus, a blessing. German poet Johann Wolfgang von Goethe in the 19th century harbored a dream that one day national literatures will phase out into world literature and by hindsight we can say his dream has come true due to largely new tools and channels conferred by the strides of science and technology, which have increasingly globalized our world into a village where human contact is made easy like instant Nestle. In the past, exchange of literature and poetry relied heavily on literary translation, and in the present day, in addition to translation, poets and writers meet and talk on a very short notice, especially in the past 30 years; the end of the cold war has brought about en masse face-to-face communications and encounters involving poets and writers operating under different social systems. A good word should be put in for such literary exchanges as they develop and evolve unprecedented in substance, depth and breadth to the extent that new trends in poetic writing quickly get spread, benefiting practitioners and professionals from unimagined quarters. This fact explains why some of the knottiest issues confronting the first-class literary critics and theorists as well as major poets and writers across the world make topics and themes for seminars, conferences, poetic festivals, etc., such as the mysterious relationship between language and poetry, the notorious intrinsic duality between content and form, consciousness and rhetoric. Such cross-cultural communications prove to be both revelatory as well as soul-searching, self-discovery. We all become better artists, if not better men and women.

Graham Mort: How do you see the role of translators and translation as we move into an increasingly globalized world?

Jidi Majia: This world is filled with poets writing in different languages but poetic translation is still important as it has played an essential role in bridging various cultures and poetic traditions, the catalyst in boosting the emergence of new poetry. Indeed, many good translations are good poetry in their own right, some being solo, others, collaboration of two or three translators. This is another way of saying that translation is at times the nursery of good poetry. Admittedly poetic translation is an attempt never from regrets, but being human spiritual adventures, poetic translation is essentially creative of the highest order and, as such deserves our respect and heart-felt gratitude. Each time I pick up a poetic translated work, a mental picture of original poet and translator arises before me struggling to row a boat across the other shore. The only trouble is that tone and sound, being such important building blocks of a poetic structure, gets lost in the process of translation. How I envy the original author who creates a thing of beauty with message, sense, tone and prosody all locked up within, yet off limits to a poet or reader who strains to peep into it or to open his ear-drums to catch the slightest shred of it. The world cannot go around without translators. Their mission is daunting but still honorable. Please pay tribute to them.

Graham Mort: Has the democratization of writing culture affected reading culture, with more people perhaps wanting to write poetry than to read it?

Jidi Majia: You characterize our age with more poets than readers and you seem to have scored a point considering that the internet has drastically lowered the threshold of the vocation of being a poet. All you have to do is sit down at your computer, move the mouse and follow your whims wherever they go before submitting them online. Even in the past without Internet, one could always poetize and put them into his desk drawers and be the sole reader of his own work bothering not a whit about finding a publisher. That being the case, I still think there are poems and poems. Certain mechanism or criteria seem to have been at work all the time separating dross from gold. There is a way of calling it the canonization, which explains, we all agree, there is a common cultural heritage composed of Homer's *Iliad*, Pushkin's *The Bronze Horseman* and Li Bai's immortal lines. No matter how advanced science and technology have evolved, it seems those criteria or standards by which great literary qualities are measured remain eternal and changeless. All this makes the concept of the democratization of writing culture more virtual than real.

Graham Mort: You've had a long and distinguished career—what motivates you to write the next poem?

Jidi Majia: I have answered this inquiry on various occasions. I will try to repeat. I guess for any serious poets, his stumbling upon a good poem could be what drives him to compose his first poem on the paper in the first place. Such a random encounter with classical and canonical poets in particular proves to be fortuitous and decisive as it has awakened me deep down to find meaning and purpose in my life. I have come into my own, as they say, that is, I discover my true self, my lifelong passion and mission. Now, earlier in my childhood, I was haunted by the stubborn issue of death, and fancy struck me one day I must learn the aptitude of reading; lucky enough, I did lay my hand at a book of selected poems of Pushkin. Eureka! I was shocked. I was pounded. I was woken up. From that moment, I was no more what I used to be. I was reborn in a sense. From Pushkin I had the revelation that poetry is not something purely private and personal. In it one can transcend one's own little ego to be used by a bigger purpose in the scheme of things. Pushkin is a model poet as he writes to be the conscience of his own nation, to be the pioneer of his own mother tongue and indeed, to be the mouthpiece of humanity in its heroic pursuit of love, freedom, equality and all beautiful ideals. That is how I track down the genesis of my poetic career.

Translated by Huang Shaozheng

Graham Mort (1955—) is a British poet who lives in the northwest of England. He is professor of Creative Writing and Transcultural Literature at Lancaster University, where he co-directs the Centre for Transcultural Writing and Research. He has worked extensively in sub-Saharan Africa, developing creative writing projects for emergent writers, also visiting Vietnam for the Asia Pacific Poetry Festival and developing a new narrative project in Kurdistan–'*Many Women, Many Words*'–with the University of Soran. Graham has published nine collections of poetry. His first book, '*A Country on Fire*' (Littlewood Press, 1986), won a major Eric Gregory award from the Society of Authors. '*Circular Breathing*' (Dangaroo Press, 1997) was a Poetry Book Society Recommendation and following the publication of '*Visibility: new and selected poems*' (Seren, 2007) a review in *The Guardian* newspaper described him as, "One of contemporary verse's most accomplished practitioners. This book perfectly exhibits the blend of formal scrupulousness, sensory evocation and intellectual rigour that has shaped his reputation." Graham also writes short fiction, winning the Bridport Prize (2007) and Short Fiction International Prize (2014) for individual stories and the Edge Hill Prize for his first full collection 'Touch' (Seren, 2010). His second collection of stories '*Terroir*' appeared from Seren in 2015. Graham's writing has been translated into more than ten languages, such as Turkish, Vietnamese and Greek.

To Create Differently: From Juan Rulfo to Octavio Paz

—A speech given at a seminar held in Peking University marking the 45th Anniversary of Sino-Mexico Diplomatic Relations

At the mere mention of the two Mexican names, Juan Rulfo and Octavio Paz, one overworked buzzword, not necessarily drained of its clear meaning, comes up instantly in my mind: creativity, or to be more precise in the present context, alternative creativity, as I trust these two Mexicans remain a legend and even something of a mystery for contemporary Mexican literature, for the Hispanic world and even beyond.

Therefore, it is utter coincidence why I chanced upon getting to know and grow eventually intimate familiarity with their work and personality, cast in such unconventional tone and artistically innovative mould. To begin with, I might say a few words about Juan Rulfo. Sure enough, I never met with him in person, a seemingly pitiable thing, although I wish that. Yet on second thoughts, one will be much consoled given this is a world populated by over 7.5 billion souls. We are not meant to meet with each of them in the average short lifespan of ours.

Yet an accidental acquaintance with Juan Rulfo turns out to be a lifelong obsession, well rewarded by a quick understanding of the various subtleties in his writing before reinforced into an informed appreciation of his greatness fed upon initial thirst and curiosity for the exotic and foreign. His two literary works, *The Burning Plain El Llano en llamas*(1953), a collection of short stories, and *Pedro Páramo*, a 1955 tale of a man discovering a ghost town, have never ceased teasing my imagination. For a literary novice of ethnic origin from China just opening up to the world in the early 1980s, Juan Rulfo was absolutely a knock-out and eye-opener experience.

Thus the first reading of his *El Llano en llamas* made me his perennial fan. In the months that followed, that slim collection of stories less than 200,000 Chinese characters became my compulsory reading and for over one year I kept the book in my pocket or in my baggage for repeated perusal. It dawned upon me there were different varieties of regionalist writings the world over and much remained to be explored and aped in the way of fellow regionalists' experimentation with technique and language. Rulfo, for one, gives his work an air of historical authenticity in his employment of a unique prose style and his seemingly bizarre characterization, and above all, in his ability to present a thoroughly Hispanic world in thoroughly Hispanic terms forerunning the Boom of the Latin American Novel that was to sweep the literary world, eastern and western countries soon.

Although critics and writers debate which authors or works fall within the regionalist genre, the following authors represent without dispute the narrative mode. Within the Latin American world, the most iconic of magical realist writers are the Ecuadorian novelist Jorge Icaza (*Huasipungo*), the Venezuelan Rómulo Gallegos (*Doña Bárbara*), the Peruvian Indigenous writers José María Arguedas (*Deep Rivers*) and Ciro Alegría (*Broad and Alien is the World*). This literary trend also includes in the African tradition eminent writers such as Chinua Achebe (*Things Fall Apart; No Lonfer at Ease; Arrow of God; A Man of the People*) and Ngũgĩ Wa Thiong'o (*Weep Not, Child; A Grain of Wheat; The River Between*).

The popularity of regionalist literature is enduring and great and the production and proliferation throughout the developing countries is extensive in the 20th century, not at all restricted to names given above who supply some of the most prototypical specimen. One thing in common is that these writers not only chronicle the contemporary social and political histories of each's country but also reflect the dominant economic plight and intellectual concerns of their own people, attaining a high artistic dimension that makes it possible for them to comment on the natural and human landscape as well as the welter of forces and causes that lead to such situations in the third world.

Regionalist writing, by its logic, will yield a group of writers who have at heart an anthropological mission: to probe into the culture of each's people by studying their folklore, linguistic peculiarities, beliefs, mores and customs and provide an insider's synthesis and interpretation other than the version supplied by outsiders. It is, in essence, an exercise at rediscovering and reaffirming one's cultural identity in a post-colonial and even post-modernist context under the implication that one can only renew one's confidence indisputably by identifying the uniqueness of individual nation's spirituality owing to their peculiar natural features.

For the third world writers, the novels were the fictional counterpart of discovering and affirming the cultural identity of individual countries in the wake of de-colonialisation waves engulfing former colonial powers in the 1950s. Yet, for Juan Rulfo, there is a stark mingling of aestheticism and social protest. Of course, he reacted in horror to the times he was living in characterized by political chaos, deprivation, incessant internecine wars, turbulence and senseless violence, but he is also one of the first to break with the lingering traces of realism-naturalism to adapt avant-garde, post-Joycean tricks to his subject matter with amazing results. His *Pedro Páramo*, a tale of a man named Juan Preciado who travels to his recently deceased mother's hometown, Comala, to find his father, only to come across a literal ghost town–populated, that is, by spectral figures. Rulfo, the subjective and anguished artist, by destroying the line of demarcation that separates what seems real from what seems fantastic, what is today, tomorrow and future, fuses both realistic and surrealistic approaches into one that is more universal in outlook and more sophisticated in style, language and temporal-spatial development. There are obvious mythical overtones in the story reminiscent of non-European views, drawn from Aztec lore, of the earth, life, individual existence, all being consonant with the ambience of the fictional town and the starkness of the narrative.

Up to this point I make bold to say, among the principal and powerful regionalist trends, Juan Rulfo might count the veritable pioneer who pushes the native theme genre to its logical extreme by breaking loose the floodgate of time, logic and concretizing the magic realism to magical heights.

No wonder Gabriel García Márquez has said that it was only his life-changing discovery that opened the way to the composition of his masterpiece, *One Hundred Years of Solitude*. He even boasted he could recite every word of the short novel by heart. Arguably mentor of the magical realism genre, Rulfo has written two books, of a high quality as good as most of those of his disciples, if not better, truly fictional milestones, winning him a place among the most prestigious practitioners of the new Latin American novel.

Pedro Páramo signals the coming-of-age of South American literature. Juan Rulfo enchants us by blazing trails in modern novel writing as he marries myth with narrative modeled on and further expanding Joycean formulas (dislocation of linear time, shifts in the narrator and his viewpoint, the probing of the psyche). He does not try to recapture the actual world with realist conventions but creates a new one endowed with magical coherence projecting onto the chaos of reality. There are scenes and situations that blur the line of life and death. There are beams of light that shoot through the unfathomable veils of the fantastic and unreal. As revolutionary as the technique, *Pedro Páramo* is not only remarkable for pacesetting the exposition through a non-linear structure, but also for its insights into the essence of what a modern novel is, affording both example for much older and more sophisticated western writers and the bulk of non-Western literary practitioners, the emerging avant garde Chinese writers in the late 1980s in particular, to follow and emulate.

How Juan Rulfo came by his magic art, of unquestioned literary merits and of universally critical appraisal remains an inexhaustible topic. Some suggest he has drawn heavily from the Indigenous Indian cosmology and philosophy in depth and great value and that he has created a fictional world so much embedded in the Aztecan symbolism, metaphor and allegory inhabited by spectral beings. To the best of my knowledge, ancient Aztecs see a unity of temporal and spatial relationship in all directions, an idea both enigmatic and revelatory.

What makes Juan Rulfo truly impressive is this: apart from being one of the first to have adopted the latest literary theories in vogue in the western country, he has blended the native belief systems and cognitive models in his fictional Comala town. He envisages an eternal loop into which time and space being linked in parallel, life, death and rebirth are cast in a process of circular motion which ushers in three different worlds, i.e., the hell, the paradise and of course the subterranean realm in Rulfo's mind.

Juan Rulfo's mythical and fantastical perspectives, as commentators aptly put it, project a sense of the complex realities by portraying "fantastical events in an otherwise realistic tone." He brings fables, folk tales, and myths into contemporary social relevance in favor of the socially and economically marginalized strata in the then Mexico, even though he seldom preaches against social abuses.

Death is not to be feared as birth and death are actually celebrated as two integral parts of a local festivity. The communal stability and sanctity of living rest on a firm conception of an afterworld called Mitran, neither hell nor paradise. Similarly, we Yi people regard death as the beginning of another life. When a Yi ceases to breathe, he sets off to a certain destination called "Symmuha", situated between the sky and the earth, an imaginary white world. To the Yi who cling to ancient mores and values, they have three souls to leave behind upon dying. One soul will remain in the cremation ground. The second will follow a special soul trail to return to the final ancestral resting place, and the last one, to be worshipped by posterity.

I owe Juan Rulfo a word of gratitude as he prompted me to embark on a long, arduous quest for identity, one to seek my tribal root and reconnect myself with my own cultural beginnings out of which I have come into my own, a truly Yi poet, aspiring to identify with and to translate faithfully the realities of Yi's life. I still remember during a visit to Mexico City, I went to the Museum of Anthropology as a token of homage to Juan Rulfo, my own cult of personality as he was known to be on the staff of the institution since 1962, or more specifically, he was in charge of the editorial department of the National Institute for Indigenous Studies, a government agency devoted to the protection and economic improvement of the primitive Indian communities. The meek, unobtrusive and low-key manner in which he conducts himself is widely deemed as epitomizing the distinctive character and temperament of the Mexican mountain people.

Among the souvenirs brought back home is a photo album, much treasured and valued, by Juan Rulfo who shot the rare photos of native Mexicans by himself. To me he is simply composing a book of fiction in the visual mode. At times lost in the reveries of the melancholic Mexican mountains and sky over and over again, my heart contracts for condolence. Sadness overwhelms me unrestrainedly.

The man and his oeuvre are for me an image, clear and erratic, like a black-and-white movie embedded in time in constant motion as he possesses the extraordinary skills and intellectual equipment much needed to symbolize and objectify his people's dilemmas, thoughts and actions whose deeper meanings remain hitherto hidden even to themselves. The combination of historiographical rigor, stylistic precision, verbal economy, and psychological insight into the generalized human misery, the plight of his country per se, has been rarely, if ever, surpassed in Latin American fiction. Apology for my possible ignorance, due to a limited reading purview on my part, I have yet to find a single writer who can match him in intellect, imagination, and succinct mode of expression in world literature.

And Octavio Paz is a ubiquitous presence, a master of modern narrative techniques in an era that sees a general boom of poetic art. He is held high in my esteem not only because he has taught me much as a poet but also because he reaffirms powerfully his faith in sanctity of life and poetry as ultimately redemptive. In fact, as he himself pointed out in an interview, he was basically an optimist: "I don't think poetry can change the world. Poetry gives us inspiration, reveals to us the secrets of heart, fragility of life, the dilemmas of intimacy. It both entertains and educates. In particular, it creates another supra-sensible world. Shows us the other face of reality. I can't live in a world without poetry because poetry salvages time and the moment: it doesn't kill it, it doesn't deprive it of its vitality."
As a poet, Octavio Paz is not the first, but he is certainly the best

writer who, by presenting an epoch-making, all-embracing picture of the social, economic and political reality, achieves heightened insights and providing important perspective on the fatal collision of the experiences of Pre-historic Latin America, Spanish colonialism and modern Hispanic world at the mercy of recurrent violence, civil strife, economic stagnation, moral and intellectual backwardness. Epic in scope, his immortal poem, "*Sun Stone*," is a hymn of praise to the Aztec Solar Calendar of Native Americans, including sophisticated discussions of philosophical and theological as well as cultural and sociological subjects on life, self, non-self, death, nothingness, existence, meaning, alienation, and sexual love. He is also one of the few masters in the 20th century who can offer sad yet affirmative views of life in all its complexity, to be admired for neither sacrificing political engagement nor compromising his artistic integrity. No wonder he once commented on politics as an art of co-existing with others and he further added that his work pointed to the side of others.

We know that the 20th century is an age swollen with social revolutions and artistic fashions at one swoop. At a time, nay, for an extended span of time, the monstrous absurdity and division of our world was such that even half of the peopling was pitted against the other half based upon a set of artifices and man-made ideologies. It was a global situation that destroyed man's spirit, his spontaneous impulses towards life, admitting no doubt, hesitation, even half measures. The name of the game was unquestioning political commitment to either one cause or another without even blinking one's eyes to the extent that most of the important poets and writers in Latin America were standing up to be counted in the leftist camping. Of course, Octavio Paz was no exception.

But our Octavio Paz, the philosopher, moralist and thinker in him, affords a detachment that made it possible to control his passionate reactions to the brutality of events in contrast to most other engaged Latin American writers. He obviously avoids taking his stand upon the insecure foundations of political or cultural collectivism. He does not easily quarrel with those who cause his anguished antagonism for antagonism's sake. With him, things and events are humanized and individualized. In a world submerged by madness, he still deems truth a greater friend above any ideological fidelity. And for truth's sake, he was strongly equivocal in condemning the massacre of students at the Tlatelolco Square on October 2, 1968 and for which he resigned his post as ambassador to India, a price paid for a noble gesture of civil disobedience.

The shift to a more rational and objective plane of vision becomes increasingly evident as Octavio Paz has been credited with singlehandedly initiating a non-partisan cultural status quo in which polemically leftist or rightist arguments were frowned upon in favor of measured, critical thinking and independent dissent in major international events. Take one example, the assassination of Trotsky that polarized the entire Western and Latin American leftists: he was the first to voice his query about the questionable character of the triumphant marches of totalitarianism at the expense of freedom of conscience even if that meant being alienated from friends like Pablo Neruda and we are told that their intimate affinity was not restored until his later years.

The two journals *Taller* and *El Hijo Pródigo* he founded, by hoisting the haughty standard of freedom of expression and humanitarianism to defy any brand of authoritarianism, have proven to be an ideal venue where different and even hostile opinions were subjected to the rational Socratic inquiry among intellectuals in the Latin American world. Adding to these vital discursive attempts are a series of seminars he hosted as to the possible scenarios of our world in a quarry and disarray, and the opinions he put forth, the prophetic accuracy and all the virtues of intellectual honesty typical of him, a knowledgeable reader will discern and detect, forms part of his more enduring legacy, radiating with metaphysical light, leaving a rich burning, enlightening flavor behind.

Octavio Paz was one of the earliest clairvoyants who realized the stupidity of unabashedly romancing with leftist approaches to all the social and political ills plaguing Latin America. Deliberate misunderstanding, if not outright ignorance, characterized the leftist perceptions of the fatal continent. To do the job, he bothered himself to pull back the veils of myth to glimpse reality and even pointed fingers at himself.

His harsh remarks did not spare the then supposedly salutary Cuban revolution and the popular military dictatorship because of their physical strength, of larger, more intricate political maneuvering, the various forms of guerrilla organizations who have had their opportunities to effect change, the reformers, theirs, yet all failing to institute development, to solve the major continental problems. He also called into question of the so-called progressiveness of the Eastern European socialist bloc. His indictment of the cynicism of the materialistic and pragmatic foreign policy advocated by the United States proved unanswerable and convincing, and perhaps, because of abundant examples of USA misbehaviors lingering longer in the public mind than its acts of benevolence. His article entitled *"The State Institution Party in 1985, at the end of its life"* was a debilitating exposé of the party's fraud at manipulating election in Chihuahua, a courageous move which further purified the Mexican public's awareness of democracy.

Here I must reserve my greatest laudation to his monumental work, not only in my estimation, of course, the immortal work of mankind, *The Labyrinth of Solitude*, personally the open sesame to enter into the Mexican soul in an instant. *The Labyrinth of Solitude* presents a vast synthesis of social, economic and political evils bedeviling his home country, remarkable for its insights into the workings of the Mexican mind. We understand Mexico better for having read this book as he imparts not only the grisly stark reality, the tormented mentality of a strife-torn nation whose intense wrestling with a hostile natural and social milieu leave them frustrated and alienated, but also unmasks an ancient people condemned to solitude through the humanistic elements of aesthetic perception and empathy, the essence of Mexican culture graphically conveyed.

In a speech, Paz reiterates the tenet fundamental to his work: "A writer is supposed to say something nobody has said before, or cares to say, or is unable to or even dare not say it. Therefore all great literary works are not electric power lines literally but so literarily in terms of their moral and aesthetic values, designed both to destroy and create. The power of a work of art to resolve and reconcile human feuds and hostility equals that of subverting reality. Great literature is merciful, healing all wounds and embalming all spiritual agonies, affirming life at its lowest ebb and flow."

I make bold to declare our great Octavio Paz means every word of what he says. His avid interest in improving human affairs, his strength of character and devotion, his daunting and incorruptible judgment are of a kind rarely joined in an ordinary being of blood and flesh, a leading and towering personality vital and significant for the course of history, greater than his purely artistic achievements.

Juan Rulfo and Octavio Paz belong to Mexico, to all the world, looked up to in universal awe and cherished in popular memory. Both iconic figures, they tell us more of humanity, credited justifiably as an alternative source of artistic creativity, dedicated to reflecting the dominant intellectual concerns and explaining to their people how and why their world came to be the way it is today. We also know more of Mexico which has little to do with change of the seasons or the return of the stars. Because of the grandness of their literary achievements as well as the seminal and revolutionary influence upon contemporary poetry and fiction the world over, the sun rising every day in the solar valley of the country called Mexico illuminates the mask of life and death, while the souls of Juan Rulfo and Octavio Paz will hover over the human scene without fail, forever on the horizon of our earth.

Translated by Huang Shaozheng

Word as Salt – an Alternative Human Paradise Made of Ligh –Transparence and Dimness of Poetic Diction

—Address at the Opening Ceremony of 2018 Zigong "Belt and Road" International Poetry Week

Compared to natural language, poetic diction belongs to a distinct category, discernibly removed to a considerable degree from daily usage in the real world. However, it is not to be inferred, in this connection, there is a clearcut and ingrained borderline between both. Rather I mean poetic language, of necessity, is at times abstract, suggestive, symbolic and cryptic. To be sure, the edifice of poetry is erected of words, one by one, one atop another, as Roman aqueducts and Egyptian pyramids, one piece laid upon or across another adroitly and seamlessly. The similitude of this poet-as-verbal-mason analogy ends where words seem to be culturally loaded to the extent, once such a poetic monument falls to pieces, the stones scattered about will respond lovingly to the human touch. Here is an occasion called forth to reflect on the primary, and indeed, primal origin and function of poetic language. A poet is, by definition, a word-conscious person committed to, even obsessed with words, so as to be empowered to give expressive, suggestive and precise shape to what he wishes to say, a shape that could do the trick of suggestion, evocation, while the poet need avoid as much as possible rhetoric and moralizing and hardly ever move into explicit generalization.

In the ultimate pooling of the Yi canonical works passed down, the pride of place goes to epics, composed without exception in parallelism or stanzas which bring with it the coming-of-age of Yi language on par with the respectable Chinese, mores, idiosyncrasies which would in good time affect every aspect of Yi culture characterized by diversity, instability and strife. Indeed, epics, not necessarily a jewel in the literal sense, but each one, verbal emerald and verbal opal, of intrinsic quality and character, collectively mark and forge a cultural heritage which nourishes Yi spirituality and give vent to local bards who vocalize and tap the rhythmical sources of their culture. It is not coincidence that linguists all surmise in some hypothetical beginning of things poetry is the only way of using language. And anthropologists basically sign up to the same notion of poetry operating both as opener of language and preserver of identity for ethnic people inhabiting the remotest corners of our globe.

As epics anchor the riddles of life amid the mundane realities of chores and toils, traditionally, epic bards within a typical Yi community perform a dual function, i.e., singers who entertain and delight by "boiling elsewhere with such a lyric yeast" as well as sages making sensible statements about the immediate world while negotiating between the secular and the divine. Thus language and poetry are believed to be linked with ritual in most of the agricultural, gathering and herding societies. Poetry, so they claim, arose at the outset in the form of magic spells invoked to fend off a famine or ensure a good harvest before being later expanded to honor forebears, explain the alteration of the seasons, life and death, and register the pathos of love forlorn lass and lad, pray away evil, comfort those who submit to bereavement. Historically, writing is subsequent to speech in that man poeticizes orally long before he writes it down. In places still inaccessible, extremely remote, where no writing system, either character or alphabet, has been evolved, oral tradition still survives for tribesmen and tribeswomen who persist in concentrating, compressing and intensifying their speech in order to render a particular experience, crystallizing it into a channel of "the spontaneous overflow of powerful feelings", centering around subjects from nature and rustic life to show their dignity and artistic validity. One of our Yi proverbs likens poems to linguistic salt. Even into today, on important occasions such as weddings and funerals, village wits still sing songs or recite poems that have call and response patterns as Negro spirituals, with lead singers setting out a line or phrase and his rival or the group responding by repeating or playing variations on it.

From the extant poetic fragments left by people of classic antiquity, we take our cues that language accounts for the making of all exemplars for poetry, of sufficient import and weight, and we must add timely such linguistic resources that go into the production of a national treasure should be deemed the cream of a national language. No wonder many a country prides itself on possessing such blessings divinely bestowed in line with the grain of their life. Indeed, the exalted views about a poet's proper place in society have been a consensus among nations "with veins full of poetic stuff" that "most needs poets and will doubtless have the greatest and use them the greatest." For the simple reason the imposing works of language by poets, executed expressively, suggestively, opaquely or evocatively, employ language as a window on experience, so varied, complex and heterogeneous, and supply an infinity of aesthetic possibilities for audience and readership.

Poets are sometimes called magicians of words, and words to poets are like wands to magicians. Flying carpets at a time and a pigeon to take wings in a wink of eye or a red fish in a tank at a spatial and temporary nodal point. For all their variety, whimsicality and creativity, poets fashion a world of their own, in its own right, which might be a far cry from what we all know and light-years removed from what we inhabit. Just like Schoenberg's innovations in atonality, sensual, spontaneous, instinctive, "sonic orgies" (as someone calls it who detests it) sound they might, they form an integral and indivisible whole, multum in parvo, and his approach, both in terms of harmony and development, has been one of the most pioneering and influential of 20th-century musical thought.

Allow me here to cite a wise passage, to the credit of a certain American poet: "A poet must be drenched in words, literally soaked in them, to have the right ones form themselves into the proper patterns at the right moment." I totally agree with him that we poets, on top of three desiderata, i.e., the conventional concern with formal properties (rhythmical or riming schemes, inner cadence), typographical arrangement (the balance and shift of the line, couplet, stanza) and ultra-modern propensity to view poetry as a linguistic construct in these toppling times, we must never toy with the ultimate problem of the diction of poetry in the whole process. It is a diction, as it were, as always, "very conscious of its power of choosing terms with an affect of precision and of combining the terms into phrases with the same affect of peculiar precision." This time-honored Homeric sensitivity and striving for lexical precision is the ultimate test of good poetry vs bad which partially accounts for the emotive obscurity and riddling intellectual opacity exemplified in the poetry of German Paul Celan, Hispanic César Vallejo, Russian Velimir Khlebnikov. Veritably the poetic artifice they have labored at and constructed is forbidding for many, a poetic Morse code, hermetically closed, to be attacked and deciphered even by professional critics, notoriously inhospitable to translators. Imaginative creations in this vein serve to indicate the complexity of the modernist temper, for a poem in essence, is not so much a sentiment, volition, passion as it is a mind, a mode of thought, perception, in short, a way of both seeing and saying. All said, they have infused their artistic complexity with a profound sense of human worth, offering occasional but important lessons, moments of illumination, however dim and obscure, brimming with the quality of affirmation that we expect from great poets.

Poetic language, or rather, verbal strands woven into a poetic fabric, to the initiated, conjures up a majestic view of a starry sky, elusive sharks in the unfathomable depths, shiny pebbles on a dry riverbed and rain drops on a flower pedal after a downpour. All of these instances provide clues as to why we delight in poetry, the sounds of words, their rhythms and rimes, as it appeals to our intellects and stimulates our imaginations by demanding that we visualize and conceptualize events, place and character outside the realm of everyday experience. For a poet of any worth, the whole span of his life is too short for wrestling with language, a hide and seek game. Sometimes he tumbles along upon it—a token of genuine blessing. Sometimes he loses any track of it. When at last he comes around to the right word, his trophy: a good poem is born. The perennial squabble remains: the limits to perception, the accessibility of truth, the nature and scope of knowing and naming.

Word are both opaque and crystal, ambiguous and mysterious. This is nothing new as our Bimos would stand testimony, dating from the infancy of mankind: chanting grandiloquently a hymn, gazing and gasping at the sprawling ranges of mountains, the sun arising and setting, and his voice being carried through fire and light to the Celestial Vaults, reverberating high and low, thither and hither. What a way of contemplating the mystery and power of the divinities and releasing cosmic energy in syn with motions of heavenly bodies! Here is another case of untranslatability, equally notoriously baffling and inscrutable as the most arcane poetic texts.

In my native place, in the Daliangshan, heartland of Yi culture, our priest figures—Bimos, still revered to ply their trade and do their business upon the human spirit, habitually say a prayer in form of poems, the best ones the Yi people can boast, "happily by the coincidence of forms that locks in the poem", the bulk of Yi poetry comprise parallelism, each divinely charged with a haunting ethos, energy, mythical might that escalates upward further and further, the ideal medium negotiating between reality and nothingness, an integral and indivisible part of our world. Our Bimos, like all great poets, enrapture us by raising their voices always, at the end, of transcendence, because they have both seen clearly and tasted poignantly the glory and misery of the miserables. The sum total of our poetic legacy, tradition and experiment, an amazing and dazzling garnering of the transparent, the cryptic, the ambiguous, the concrete, the abstract, the metaphysical, the symbolic, the surreal, the elusive, the accessible, the pat, discloses to us this vital truth intimately and distinctly.

Translated by Huang Shaozheng

Narcissistic Self—Seeking Is Not the Sole Responsibility of a Decent Poet
—*Acceptance speech at the Awarding Ceremony of Tadeusza Micińskiego Prize*

I am, indeed, overwhelmed with the award given to me today, veritably a true literary distinction which leaves a good excuse for revisiting the realm of belle lettres mostly akin to my personal slant in the affairs of the world and in matters of the heart. Forget any mistrust on my part of the normal function of language when I fumble for words of gratitude as a proper act of response at this moment. I surmise a narrative of a certain length might do the trick. All said, all the audience today should be fully acquainted with my special affection for Polish letters.

My mind returns to an oration delivered by one of the greatest Polish poets the 20th century can offer, i.e., Czeslaw Milosz, the moralist, at Jagiellonian University entitled "Counter the World with Polish Poetry", a speech of enormous ethical and artistic importance, both as an incentive to his counterparts and as fair warning to world poets, wherein he set forth his unequivocal position to the effect that "Polish writers shall never extenuate themselves to their predecessors and posterity in matters of the mind, the cross of their trade." With this self-inflicted obligation and shout of call to responsibility emitted, he demystifies any claim of a literature free of commitment and he speaks for us all that poetry must always serve a cause and for this alone I bow to no one in my admiration for his poetry and his personality, and indeed, the Polish poetry in general.

A cursory glance at the 20th century world literature onward will lead us to the fact, no matter how grudgingly allowed by some, that

Poland, together with East Europe and Middle Europe, has startled and fascinated the world by the quality of imagination and language that was called upon and brought to bear upon both national and human experience as well as by the wealth of exemplary Polish men and women of letters arising out of their sufferings and out of the lessons they derive for us. Equally or more deserving of credit, it could be argued, is the exceptional accomplishments of Russian geniuses of Silver Age, as ever, standing on the high ground of artistic integrity and moral duty. For in the past 100 years or so, the great panoply of Polish poets, in particular, taking up the yoke upon them unflinchingly, trapped in circumstances which would easily crush and destroy any other human group but adduce superhuman virtues, have emerged from the morass of "moronic apathy, drunken torpor and morbid, wounded nationalism" as a result of national misfortunes, to come out with works of art, of refined taste, tender irony and mingled pathos, sometimes marked by apocalyptic or humorously macabre visions. Anybody familiar with the terrible fate of Polska, again and again, partitioned by both strong and even weaker neighbors, the Teutons, Turkey, Muscovy, Prussia, erased from the map of the world for over 120 years, will knowingly reckon with, arguably the more or less permanent trait of Polish letters, i.e., "a strong emotional moralism" fed obviously by Christian ethic. What is offered is nothing short of a triumph of distillation of crushing experiences of Poles in particular or of the existential depths visited practically by all of us nowadays. In comparison, any rhetoric's-for-rhetoric's-sake poetry, stripped of such human caring would still look pale and lack weight and substance.

Beyond dispute, the universal recognition of Polish poetry lends itself, in the flux of literary history, to the cardinal thesis that poetry has no meaning if contained within the bounds of narcissistic indulgences and exaggerations and this is not to deny the importance of a poet to legitimately wrestle with falsifying emotions by "concern with form" and due effort at "unsentimental purity of things". But Milosz's treatment of the basic theme of Polish poetry remains valid: "the tension between a poetic dedication to form and compassion for human suffering." This award, named after Tadeusz Miciński, who earns our respect for his expressionist fascination with originality and innovation, has never disavowed, indeed, he has fulfilled preeminently the wishes of all Polish poets for a balance between an all-out social protest and faith in man as well as pursuit of artistic excellence.

We confront a world still chaotic and full of incongruities. Complaints of its spiritual poverty as well as paucity of good poetry are as old as the art itself. This heart-rending state of affairs, buttressed by a logic of material and technology holding sway the spirit, the fad of the 21st century, constitutes the biggest reason to call forth our most vigorous efforts to keep pace with the age as poets.

Carried away, as we are, by waves of technological breakthroughs, past experience sometimes surprises the pessimists who foresee the durable effects of modernization. With an awesome array of new gadgets at our disposal, robots, genes engineering, cloning, cloud computing, internet, superconductivity material, digital currency, there seems to be a place for euphoria, triumphant mankind and exuberant poets enveloped within the intricacy of syntax and deconstructed lexicon, who could "perform a spontaneous dance without recourse to compulsive justifications". Yet the images of Syrian imps screaming audibly over the loss of their mothers on the debris of their former cozy homes inundate our TV screens, which compels our unkempt attention, a timely reminder we are still situated between the holocaust of the last war and the atomic devastation, a danger not exactly imminent, but still lurking ominously somewhere ahead of us, for the existing arsenal of atomic bombs, we are told, can still decimate humans and all the sentient beings thousands of times.

Milosz rightly admonishes us that the act of writing poetry is an act of faith. Our activity is certainly tantamount to an offense if we juggle with poetry and fail to produce poems that rival the immortal pieces of the old in defense of human civilization and exemplify the attempt to resist the growing disparity in the cultural and economic life in the world.

Translated by Huang Shaozheng

Poets Empowered by a Mysterious, Dark and Burning Sound
—*Address at 2019 4th Xichang Qinghai Silk Road International Poetry Week*

> *Goethe, who in speaking of Paganini hit on a definition of the Duende: "A mysterious force that everyone feels and no philosopher has explained."*

To speak personally for a moment, one place, in this troubled world, calls me home; one place recharges my spirit and fires my imagination each time I find my way back. I mean Greater Liangshan, "the most favored spot on earth", my native place and ancestral home. In that holy place, as if I drink there from a well, I am repossessed by that mysterious power, a dark electricity, the Duende, as Lorca termed it, "from which," he said, "comes the very substance of art." Duende is the edge original art is made on; it is the darkness in the art that fashions enduring poems; it is the artistic iconoclasm fresh performance embodies. It is the newness that poetry sometimes makes. Most of us poets have now and then neared that source—have found ourselves turning out miraculous lines or poems that surprise even us who make them. Duende is the source good poems issue from; we know it "when they hit us hard, teach us, reach home". There comes sometimes a moment like a flaring of truth, when words, no longer merely ours, are burned into gems—a chemistry performed, an alchemy conjured, in the poet's throat and in her writing hand. In such rare moments, Lorca's Duende attends, walks us behind her into the promise of "something newly created, like a miracle", which it is our task to form. The miracle is not so much the poem we sometimes pull off; it is how the Duende feels—elusive, mysterious, murky, oracular.

I love this esoteric concept of the Duende; it accords with the animism at the heart of Yi culture. We Yi people have inhabited the hard and stubborn mountain ranges called the Greater Liangshan for many thousands of years, and our contributions to the Chinese civilization—to world civilization—are countless and varied. Anomalous among the big family of China, we are an animistic people: our places are legended, animate; our culture's ethos is Occultist; our priests—Bimos or shamans—still perform the eternal task of interceding between the people and the spirits of the earth, of the heavens, making peace between the present and the past.

Bimos are our spiritual and ceremonial leaders; they are still charged with mediating between the secular and the divine; they are esteemed as the bearers of spiritual wisdom essential and inherent to our people. All ancient spiritual practices are rooted in nature, and the chief work of the Bimos is naturally to waken and conserve the people's connection with the natural world. Greater Liangshan—the place and its people—is as dynamic as it is enduring. Although modernization and globalization menace and encroach, although modernity makes deafening inroads, in no other place is spiritual practice so entwined with everyday civil life. Even while urban Yi folk stride into the 21st century, still you'll find our Bimos doing what they've done since the Bronze Age—performing rites that ensure the safe passage of the deceased to heaven; chanting prayers in deep voices. In more sequestered places, villages one only reaches by foot, you might still witness a village funeral, you might take note of sacrificial branches and twigs placed carefully on the ground, although they seem scattered at random—laid out below to mirror the constellations above.

What appears to be a reshuffling of attitudes and lifestyles in many Yi communities is mostly surface. Deeper, although change is taking place on massive scale, with smart phones, laptops and an awesome array of gadgets woven into the fabric of Yi life, the ageless verities and loyalties remain; they run in the veins of the Yi. The Muse or some Angel above is the usual suspect poets turn to explain what drives them to the page. But we would do well to heed Lorca's Duende exhortation that to deserve and perhaps endure the Duende, one must never cease from the struggle to inhabit one's self—our real selves that slumber to be awakened, the ones we barely recognize—because we are so often far alienated from our racial roots. At times when I am in the reverent presence of Bimos chanting a prayer, perhaps in a trance, I see before me, the shaman's words floating like flames, and this vision leads me to a door that opens on the real rationale for being a poet—or continuing to be one. To make a poem is a call from beyond, made of words, but encapsulating something powerful, but given only to one who's made a leap of imagination—one might almost say of faith. It is a power that will lead you outside or push you inside yourself; it will wake you wider; it will infuse you—intoxicate, perhaps—with an urge to create, to seek "answers for unformed questions, to stop time, to understand the undecipherable, to reach out for a kind of magic". It is Lorca's "miracle".

The genesis of Lorca's concept of Duende was the Gypsy tradition of the "Deep Song", a predecessor to Flamenco in Lorca's native Andalusia. During his sojourn in New York in the years of 1929-1930, Lorca involved himself in American folk traditions of jazz, blues, and spirituals, which brought him to the proposition: the "dark sounds"—canto jondo—and their relationship to life and art. For me, a Chinese equivalent of the Duende, a better translation of it, maybe, might be soul force, which we Yi people identify as the essence of our culture.

Marina Ivanovna Tsvetaeva, the great Russian poet, once labored to expound a similar theme in her article dedicated to Vladimir Mayakovsky and Boris Pasternak: "Yes, Mayakovsky will be exhausted thematically some day, but his power will survive and stay as earth will survive and stay, once and for all. As for Pasternak, his action resembles that of a dreamer. He plunges us into him, underneath him, in him. We understand him by shunting him aside and we are drawn to him irresistibly by not attempting to understand him."

One of the giants of 20th century British poetry, Ted Hughes pinpoints things in common between a poet and a witch—a prophet's vision, psychic power, guardianship of the racial memory, divine rights and a status assigned by tradition or chosen by supernatural beings, and he extols the various virtues of his brilliant predecessor Irish Yeats in superlatives: "Yeats is suffused with Irish national spirit and supernatural ethos and folklore and legends populate his poems. By donning the mysterious mantle, he builds a spectacular aim in life and in poetry: revive the Irish energy, rehabilitate the deposed pantheon of Irish divinities and reforge the unconquerable Irish soul."

Countless encounters with it, hard facts I can't account for otherwise, convince me the arch-reason that hovers like a haze of wisdom around poetic writing is that elusive pitch of being Lorca calls the Duende, which others might name the soul, the psyche, the subconscious or the unconscious. We know it's there; we feel it working in our hearts and days as surely as Galileo Galilei felt the earth moving underfoot 400 years ago against prevailing orthodoxies. One is as powerless to know when, or how, or even why it strikes as one is to predict a mood or call up a dream. But this rare pitch of being, this way of the spirit, is what sustains a poet and lends him a voice to say the unsayable, to name the unnamable, to discern the undiscernible. This dark and burning sound, that the otherness the Shaman divines, is the exhilarating mystery that surrounds and enables the profoundly human activity of making poems.

Translated by Huang Shaozheng

Forces Hidden in Poetry: Let's Make a Rendezvous with Tradition!
—Address at the 6th Qinghai Lake International Poetry Festival

Tradition is arguably one of the most important human institutions astride both good poetry and history. Then in what way does our poetic tradition let us into the secret of great poets? Our poetic tradition, as it stands, can be likened to a river, driblets at their glacial source, gathering many a streamlet before forming into a mighty current, rushing passionately over rapids and past gorges, down through a staggeringly long time. Or they can still be seen as the first note of the symphony score of a myth, prayer at the tongue tip of our Bimos (Yi priests or shamans). The idea is that no matter how much shrouded in antiquity of which the beginning of tradition, so far as our ears give due audience, we will be much reassured of the message, words of nature, speaking to us out of the dense darkness that it is still pretty much around, dying really hard.

Tradition, if anything, lives in our language all the time, which, being a special human memory, is as indestructible as the most stubborn trace left by humans on earth. Indeed, no other power can boast of equal omnipotence. Historians, by fathoming the depth of this undercurrent of language, by piecing together innumerable evidences unearthed, countless artifacts and cultural relics scattered around the globe, conjure up the Neolithic sociological patterns of various migrating tribes and herds. While mountains and oceans have risen and drained away, human remains buried deep have turned into mulberry fields or fossilized, the baggage upon your back is no more a pack, millions and millions of years have elapsed during which your clear remembrance becomes a legend, and no amount of positivistic research and archeological reconstruction will tell the truth for sure: the truth about where we in the first place launch forth in life and wander widely asunder in the world. Only at this moment, halting at the crossfire of reasoned speculation, all the elements of which the science is sure and frankly mysticism, we content ourselves with the reassuring oracle made of words that suggest some clues so as to appease our inquisitive turn of mind.

Ever since the beginning of things, human travels fall into two categories: mental and physical. I must observe, of course, even physical wandering that I am talking here does not merely carry the Darwinian sense of linear progression. Human travels, mentally speaking, have utter metaphysical undertones, and because of this, I trust what is encrypted in language is far more a metaphor of eternity illumined by the torch through time.

Tradition is both a state of mind and a mode of thinking and if it is set forth more distinctly with ontological implication, as to encompass mankind at large, it is the universal mental processes prevalent in all civilized lands, functioning in all aspects of social life, from philosophizing in the ivory tower to daily intercourse of ordinary folk, indeed, so deeply embedded in the unconscious of most of us (We are such unconscious people!). Our world has certainly become more worldly. Some mighty invisible forces are at work making havoc on manners, mores and customs of honest days of yore—when as yet I only believed them to be all that poets had painted them;—"being gradually worn away by time, but still more obliterated by modern fashion." But in this season of irreversible change, tradition, with a pleasing vengeance, asserts its immortality most vigorously, as tenacious as our gene chromosomes, empowering us to see the starry sky rarely seen by others, to sing the hymns which are Greek to everybody not of our paternal home, and more important, tradition-conscious, we have been able to keep watch on the returning dawn of another tomorrow. Tradition as human spirituality, I claim proudly as core ICH (intangible cultural heritage) of our Yi people above all else. I plead ignorant when asked whether there is a poetic tradition of higher antiquity than ours, but this much I can tell you for sure: once we have come to grips with the essence of our glorious poetic tradition, we will become the vanguard to usher in a new phase of artistic innovation.

We often speak of modernity as approbative or synonymous of the frontier of modern poetry but we might remind ourselves that modernity is as inevitable as breathing, since we are all literally living in this modern age and that we should be none the worse for failing to record what happens under our very noses as chronicler and eyewitness, simply because we cannot live elsewhere, say the Tang or the Pericles' time, fully aware of the immortal pieces left to us by a Li Bai or Homer, all super beings "radiant with the emanations of their genius", secure in the quiet recesses of the bosom of time in perennial renown. For good or bad, "it is still a turn-up of a die, in the gambling freaks of fate", whether we do our part or fail in our ultimate capacity as poets of our age. One of the Chinese poets, not necessarily a prophet, whose name escapes my memory at the moment, is remembered as saying something to the effect: "The past five decades could well be termed the most amazing period in this country's history as it sees nothing short of a revolution being materialized." Shame on us if we only sit idle decrying economic growth, deploring galumphing consumerism or fretting about urbanization. It simply does behoove us, aside from the excitement of creation and the feeling of achievement, to translate the sensory impressions of such unprecedented mind-boggling, striking events, external and internal, into beauty on a verbal plane.

Granted poetry has always kept company of us, I must confess my firm faith in poetic possibilities in galore for each generation born into every period in history. The world of poetry is wide and rich, there is enough room in it for every person who wants to poeticize. Barriers of temperament, talent, artistry and bottleneck in ambition are natural and should be expected. But a whole-hearted zest to take risk to be frontrunners is not flimsy daydreaming. It is a goal, nay, a reality, all of a sudden, sprung unto us and we feel it palpably as the world is spinning under our feet with all its motion and velocity. Hence, poetic innovation in this era of dazzling alterations is no more a subject that invites discussion and hypothesis, it is a reality confronting us, each of us who will willingly renounce the relative security of the present niche we have earned and deserved in society for the unpredictable life of dare-to-shine-or-perish innovator.

I have given my speech the title of "Forces Hidden in Poetry", because, shorn of innovation in new style and diction, we are leading to nowhere in our attempt to have the faintest inkling of where the hidden forces lie and by which way we will get to the forefront. Innovation is the ordeal of good poetry. New trends or even reversal in style and diction sometimes don the garb of bewildering mysticism to the point of something like a mumbo jumbo, but it is an effort worth making, should be deemed norm rather than abnormity, and indeed, the yardstick by which one can tell good art from something like a fad to be soon lost in the sand, or a much exalted school totally saturated, on the verge of being repudiated en masse, "victim of a new unforeseen reversal in stylistic innovation". The ideal for poetic innovation is to create new forms and come out with new style and new diction, which stand both for a new set of symbols and metaphors in an age calling forth drastic stylistic experiment much in arrear of material progress.

I have dwelt upon possible ways of identifying these UFO in poetry, because, as it is one of the most sacred duties of each good poet, so is it the overarching office of poetry. All those refusing to be weak, limited artistic personalities must necessarily make the leap into the unknown, eternally unattainable of poetic writing. Such bouts might prove futile for a gigantic enterprise, a faint glimmer in a murky room, or even darkness as reflection of light and gold. Poetry sets no front-line or limitation on the still mysterious nature of human creativity. To truly discover such a one, we might as well turn ourselves into logs, bricks, barbwire, cement, ammunition and forge our forward position. Good or bad lot, a poet innovates ultimately by dating and romancing with tradition again, which will, like a holy flame, illumine the road ahead of him.

A good poet invariably comes to reckon with these unforeseen forces and his growth, paradoxically, is measured by the extent to which he retreats into the tradition of his own people, which will goad and sustain him to awareness, understanding and eminence.

Translated by Huang Shaozheng

Poetry, a Tribute to Love, an Arsenal Against All Violence

—*A keynote address delivered at the Sino-Czech Roundtable on Literature on the Commemoration of the 70th Anniversary of Sino-Czech Republic Cultural Exchange and the Independent Czechoslovak State Day*

Today marks the 70th anniversary of the founding of the People's Republic of China, the 70th anniversary of Sino-Czech Republic Cultural Exchange, and the Independence Day of Czech. Upon this important occasion, I am very happy to join with you, as a poet from China, at the Sino-Czech Roundtable on Literature. Please therefore allow me to convey my best and most sincere wishes to each of you.

I visited the Czech Republic twice, the first time upon invitation of my Czech publisher in spring 2016 for the launch and first public reading of my poetry anthology *Flames and Words*, in fact a co-translation by Czech sinologist Zuzana Li and poet Jaromír Typlt. Therefore I believe I am not a stranger to your country. Of course, prior to this I had already had another anthology published in the Czech Republic, entitled *Time*, a rendition from its English version. And shortly in autumn 2018, I had the privilege to be invited to the 28th annual Prague Writers' Festival (PWF), an occasion upon which I participated along with a Swedish poet Cletus Nwadike and Iranian poet Abolghasem Esmailpour—the latter of whom also happened to be translator of my anthology in Persian—in a roundtable themed "The Evils of Living" hosted by Michael March, founder of the PWF, where I had the opportunity to field some questions from the audience. My Czech visit, especially that to the world-renowned city of Prague, left indelibly good impressions upon me.

At this moment there is something which I hope to say to all of you, that it was in fact at a much earlier time when a fascination with Prague as an enchanting city began to burgeon in me, along with an irresistible longing to visit it someday. That was when I chanced upon a passage by Friedrick Wilhelm Nietzsche, the legendary German philosopher who put it beautifully in parallelism: "When I seek for a word to express my love of music, I find Vienna; when I seek for a word to express my idea of mystery, Prague comes to my mind." And if my memory serves me right, it is the German literary giant Johann Wolfgang von Goethe who famously defines the city as, "the most beautiful jewel in the crown of the globe."

Prague fascinates me yet in more ways than one. For one thing, to me, a passionate amateur of classical architecture, Prague is nothing short of a de facto museum of architecture in every sense of the term, home to architectural legacies of an endless long list of historical periods and feathering a large variety of fashions and tastes, most noticeably the Baroque and the Gothic, earning the city an unshakable and most prominent place in the architectural history of the Continent. To me, an inveterate aficionado of classical music, the city was birthplace to Antonín Dvořák, Bedřich Smetana, and Leoš Janáček, all of whom great composers, whose masterpieces, after repeated listenings, still hold me captive even to this day, casting me spellbound whenever the melodies spring up. Among their masterpieces, the most thought-provoking is perhaps Dvořák's Symphony *No.9*, more famously known as New World Symphony, which for a time would render me pensive and lost in imagination, leaving me with a belief that music can revitalize a people's soul on a separate place of existence from ours; a symphonic poem by Smetana, *Má vlast*, or *My Country*, revealed to my sight every immortal thing possibly found in music, brought to life by notes and melodies, which did not simply fade away, but rather continued their vital existence in the depths of time; the revelation and shock incited and triggered by Janáček's orchestral rhapsody *Taras Bulba* and his *Sinfonietta* far exceeded any abstract tome of philosophy I had ever chanced upon, for they had instilled in me a knowledge that oftentimes it was from the elements of native languages and folk songs that soul-stirring melodies were best distilled, a fact which must have also hold true from such moral sentiments as caring for the underdogs to make their voices heard, a sentiment striking me in sympathetic awe of the tongues spoken by every downtrodden peoples worldwide, including the Yi tribe to which I belong.

Myself being a fan of Goethe's concept of "world literature", especially more than a full century after his passing, and despite the ongoing wipeout of cultural differences resulting from cultural immersions happening at an ever-increasing pace, more and more are awakening to the goodness of multicultural preservation, cultural diversity, and the great humanist traditions, which remain the unshakable cornerstones of this "world literature". The concept of "national literatures" has already collided, and now overlaps with "world literature", a universalized concept, prompting us to redefine the latter, of which Czech literature is just an epitome. The epoch-making expressionist writer Franz Kafka, primogenitor of modernist literature, who lived in Prague all his life, could be said to have already become a cultural symbol of the city. This is to say nothing of an earlier time period, when the emergence of a big batch of eminent writers on the literary scene of the country as early as the 20th century, whose coming-of-age both elevated the status of Czech literature among European intelligentsia, and made palpable to the world the looming Czech literary presence. Among these writers, we are most familiar with Jaroslav Hašek, Vladislav Vančura, Karel Čapek, Václav Havel, Milan Kundera, Ivan Klíma, and in addition to them, Bohumil Hrabal, out of heartfelt admiration for whom I took some time out of my hectic schedule here to drive over for a special visit to his forest bungalow, to which he had retired from the world for the sole purpose of writing; and then to his graveyard, shrouded with a like air of simple austerity in which he had led his life, a graveyard which he chose for himself, now scattered with doll cats brought halfway across the world by admirers of all nationalities, for we know cats had been his best friends—in fact, he had even kept food in his forest bungalow for these close confidants of his!

As an intellectual explorer fascinated with linguistics, linguistic anthropology, and semiotics, Prague charms me, for it was here that the genius Roman Jakobson, undoubtedly a trailblazer in structuralist thought and movements, who founded the Prague School, became the very first thinker to establish linkages between structural linguistics and poetic criticism, revealing a mysterious effect of metaphor and metonymy in poetry, a pioneering intellectual achievement making possible all the subsequent explorations in and experimentations with language. It was also Jakobson who, capitalizing on linguistic and rhetorical discoveries in poetry, ventured to undertake in-depth analyses of the works of Velimir Khlebnikov, the Russian futurist poet.

As a poet myself, I cannot deny the extraordinary zeal I have for Czech poetry, many of which I have read while still in college, including the long poem *May* by Karel Hynek Mácha, pioneer of poetry of a new era, whose works themed around romantic love, expressing the earnest wishes of a people yearning for national rebirth. Most importantly, proceeding from human nature, he hoisted individual sentiments up to the majestic heights of human morality. In a periodizing poets in contemporary Chinese poetry, I can be loosely pigeonholed as one who came of age in the 1980s, the heyday of China's open door policy; which is to say, foreign influences including Czech poets constitute a sizable part of my poetic and intellectual pedigree. They include, but are not limited to, contemporary poets such as Vítězslav Nezval, the master surrealist, under whose influence countless Czech poets adopted the novel poetical assertions against asceticism and rationalism, not to mention his infusing late-surrealism with the latest values and attitudes.

The poet Jaroslav Seifert extolled beauty all his life, such as in the following verse: "Heaven may be just / A smile we've been waiting for so long / Two lips softly calling our name / And then for a brief moment it was dizzying / The existence of hell is forgotten". These lines moved me so much after one reading that, whenever upon retrospection, I still feel a thrill through me as the first time I stumbled upon them. During my Czech visit, at one time we rushed to his graveyard, arriving there no sooner than the dusk had befallen his hometown, when the graveyard warden was just about to lock up the heavy iron gates. In no time did I dart out from the car, screaming

"Jaroslav Seifert! Jaroslav Seifert!" at him desperately. No, I did not know a single word of Czech, yet he must have understood what I meant, for he unlocked the gates, and let in our group of visitors who came all the way from the other end of the globe. Oh, Vladimír Holan, the hermetic poet who had stayed on Kampa Island in Prague, whose terse and witty epigrams abounded with esoteric philosophy and metaphors, whose poetry was shrouded in mysticism of meditations over life and death, existence and non-existence, such as this: "Oh yes / I love life / that's why I sing so much about death / without death / life would be so cold / with it / life could be imagined / and that's why it's so absurd…" It was Holan who opened my eyes to the true meaning of life which, of course, was at the same time not without an twinge of the absurd. O, master poet Miroslav Holub., arguably more accomplished in poetry than medicine which he also practiced—since viewed within the grander scope of time, any spiritual creation is unfathomably unperishable and malleably extendible—who in the famous masterpiece of the verse *Galileo Galilei* had uttered this: "I / Galileo Galilei / in the church of Mineweina / in a shirt / on thin legs / under the pressure of the world / Me / Galileo Galilei / in a low voice / for the children / for the movers / for the sun— / In a low voice / at last… / The earth / indeed/is spinning around under my feet" and who has made me understand that, should poetry at any moment cease to be thought-provoking and to sustain human suffering, it would at that very moment be stripped of all its raison d'etre. During my Czech visit, I had my friend Jaromír Typlt prepare for me a disk containing poems for recitations by the most important contemporary Czech poets. All these hectic years, I would often take some time off to listen to Vítězslav Nezval, František Halas, Holan, Seifert, whose works and voices were always there with me, and for me, bestowing me some touching moments of solace and of encouragement, and upon my bedraggled heart, mind, and soul feelings which could never have really been shared with and felt by anybody else. In a sense, no great poet who has passed away would "wander in Death's shade", but instead they live on forever and ever.

The Czechs are known for their magnanimous outlook, and for their good sense of humour, due to the fact that Central European people had been repeatedly harassed and oppressed by surrounding powers and such historical fate goes beyond the geopolitical into the cultural sphere, as the Bohemian spirit which throughout history has braved the vicissitudes of time, now an inseparable part of the Czech cultural tradition as seen in the voluminous creations by contemporary Czech poets who have, as we can see, created a safe haven of words, a shelter from the violence so palpably felt in their own lives and those of others around them. Out of love for mankind and for everything beautiful in this world, with stunning forbearance and stamina they have confronted the abject misery and the most intolerable hardships, that is to say, under the draconian rule of the Nazis, when nevertheless their poetry retained its power of irony, appreciation of life, individual character, and human dignity, which despite the ups and downs have nevertheless been passed down in their works. From many compassionate poems on human suffering, we can see the power of poetry at work and at its best, carrying out its mandate as the guardian keeper of human morals and lofty ideals. Anyone studying closely the Czech history of modernization will find that for this nation, poetry has always been with the common people, each and every word like a shining metal bullet, penetrating lies and hypocrisies with its all-conquering power of truth. With their unique and richly individualistic poetical expression, this variety of poetic genius who began to make the Czech poetic stage in the 1930s made visible to us the enormous role which poetry played over more than half a century in helping humanity strive for happiness, testifying for us to the zeitgeist, restoring us to moral dignity, and more. Our history and reality have told us that poetry is not merely a tribute to love, but also a most treasurable arsenal against all violence.

Translated by Huang Shaozheng

The Meaning, Dissemination and Inner Secrecy of Poetry
—*Address at the seminar of 3rd International Poetry & Liquor Conference*

Czeslaw Milosz, back in 1990 wrote an article entitled *Against Incomprehensible Poetry*, in which he made explicit some of the tacit implications in his view of poetry to the effect that he should be deemed on the side of those who hanged on to virtues of poetic accessibility and traditional poetic ambition about spiritual consolation or social effectiveness or duty. Basically he believes a poem, like any artistic creation, is of supreme human import while eschewing largely the obscurantist and elitist stance, in vogue among some quarters, prioritizing opacity that characterizes some extreme poetic experiment of forms to the extent the more incomprehensible, the better the poem, as if non-communicability is an absolute good.

True, from our retrospective position, it makes most sense to see innovation and tradition as existing in a symbiotic relationship. Experiments in the name of a diminished aesthetic or "purest forms" and forays into the secrecy, metaphoricity and symbolicity of poetry have pullulated and sustained generations of poets that enable them to emerge into notoriety, in a spate of poetic postures available as the legacy of post-symbolism, surrealism, futurism and modernism. These ventures have importantly reshaped the contours of contemporary poetry and colored our discourse in poetic discussions. I do see eye to eye with one key aesthetic assumption of reader criticism as to how thousands of readers, historical or implied, join with a poet "to help the text mean". Such aesthetic principles hearken to Velimir Khlebnikov, a poets' poet lauded by Mayakovsky, both iconic figures of the Russian Futurist movement. In his work, Khlebnikov experimented with the Russian language, drawing upon its roots to invent huge numbers of neologisms, and finding significance in the shapes and sounds of individual letters of Cyrillic. He even developed "an incoherent and anarchic blend of words stripped of their meaning and used for their sound alone" known as Zaum. The result was that he supplied the readers two linguistic systems, one for public reading, the other, sheer encrypted code to be broken by poets only.

As a pioneer of the structural analysis of language, which became the dominant trend in linguistics during the first half of the 20th century, Roman Jakobson was among the most influential linguists from the Prague School and he also became a pivotal figure in investigating poetry by adapting insights from semiotics etc. Jakobson, fascinated with the idea of poetry as autonomous, theorized convincingly about what intrinsically undergirded poetic art by positing binary opposites, i.e., poetic diction vs ordinary diction before unraveling the uniqueness and complexity of poetic idiom. To sum, Jakobson meant to "purify poetry of all that is not poetry," ensuring us to assess the aesthetic unity of the poem with a tool by which we could separate chaff from the wheat with ease.

It is hardly surprising that literary history is littered with unpredictable trajectories of poets oscillating between a commonsense faith in the autonomous, coherent self to represent both self and world in transparent language and a corresponding skepticism concerning metaphysical claims and openly rhetoric and opaque use of language. Contemporary poetry is more meaningfully seen in many ways as a larger continuum, at once linked and segregated by this set of seemingly contradictory dualities. A master like Czeslaw Milosz is highly various and subtle in his rhetorical kit and despite a progressive stylistic thinning out, he remains a staunch skeptic of the so-called "pure poetry" shunning any "metaphysical claims" or "epic imperative".

By temperament, in the face of a world that has so tragically gone wrong, I feel quite comfortable to subscribe to Milosz's concern with "the impact of history upon moral being, the search for ways to survive spiritual ruin in a ruined world", deeply aware of the viability of the claims made by modernists' scrupulous devotion to the craft of poetry. Yet, this does not mean that a poet, in his effort to register the world beside and beyond the self and to be constantly at the cutting edge in technique and thought, has to make virtue of obscurity, bad organization, neglect of logic, intent on "his own world and his own forms" at the expense of increasingly limiting poetry's terrain. Easy legibility, caused by mass literary and mass journalism, should always be guarded against as a baneful influence in poetry. We as poets do need some external or inner reality to refer to or even self-refer to, yet we should also transcend the triviality of material reality if not to submit our work to the astringency of "pure poetry", since poetry has its genuine value primarily in "the sphere of the intangible and the imaginary" as well as of the social and the ethical—a sphere different from other arts where a high-minded practitioner is expected to create beauty by reinvigorating language, both chaste and creative, to discard conventions outmoded and invent new ones instead, and last but not least, to affirm the value of human life, no matter how hard. A truly great poet looks to me like a magician teetering on the high tension wire, assured of all the hazards, still safe and secured.

To conclude, I feel tempted again to quote Pablo Neruda, one of the Latin American poetic giants of the 20th century, when he discloses to us most intimately the ultimate recipe for his crowning achievement: "If a poem is intelligible to everybody, it won't be a good one for sure; likewise, if a poem remains enigmatic to all, it is a bad one without fail."

The subject of the meaning of poetry, its dissemination, and its inherent secrecy will continue to engage and challenge the community of poets—arguably the eternal charm of the craft of poetry for decades, perhaps, centuries, to come. That means we must content ourselves wrestling relentlessly with this perennial tension embedded in the fundamental aesthetic premises upon which both modern poetry and poets' vocation rest.

Translated by Huang Shaozheng

Let Poetry Empower Us Strongly for Marching Toward Tomorrow and Future
—An Address on 2020 Kritya Poetry Festival, India

First of all, I would like to extend congratulations for the inauguration of Kritya Poetry Festival and best regards toward all dear friends attending this Festival through internet videos! At present, all human beings face a special moment that we are devoting every effort to fight against COVID-19 virus, the common enemy of humankind. It is a pleasure to see that in such a difficult time, poetry still plays a role of encouraging people to march toward tomorrow, that we poets are also not absent in this battle. We are especially proud that in order to promote human peace and a better future of this planet, we poets speak up for justice in various countries and areas, fighting resolutely against all evil forces impeding the establishment of understanding, harmony and better relationship among different civilizations and nationalities, particularly condemning the arising clamour of racism, Neo-Nazism and terrorism. I believe that as long as the poets of the whole world unite and cooperate with each other, our poetry must produce the mighty spiritual power, so that all human beings will be full of confidence and courage on the journey to tomorrow and future. Currently, the virus wreaks havoc on the world, and humankind is hovering between exceptional arduousness and advancing to tomorrow of hope. Please allow me to recite a part of my long poem, *Split-Open Planet*, to express my tribute to the lofty spirit of human beings who have never yielded to any disaster.

O, humankind, this is the time disinfectants flow along national borders.
It's the time when you'll be next if the person beside you gets it.
It's the time when dissolving time and thirsty arrows are in a race.
It's the time when we mock others and can't do good by ourselves.
It's the time when that zealous ice is carving the raging inferno.
It's the time when the earth and people simultaneously don facemasks.
It's the time when eagles in the sky fight with red foxes in the wilderness.
It's the time when all the boulevards and public squares fall silent.
It's the time when children can only imagine the ocean from beside the window.
It's the time when angels in white and the god of death approach the abyss.
It's the time when lonely seniors will devour despair in one gulp.
It's a time when it's safer to stay home than it is to go out.
It's the time when the outstretched hand in the throat of vagabonds is the hungriest.
It's the time when advocates for humanitarian aid are greater than ideology.
It's the time when urban tribal peoples are forced to return to the countryside.
It's the time when the earth, sea and sky pay their respects to living beings.
It's the time when doves fly out from cut-open veins.
It's the time when Italian tears blur Chinese eyes.
It's the time when moans in London make Spanish guitars whimper.
It's the time when New York nurses cry with God.
It's the time when lies and the truth appear and disappear on the internet.
It's the time when Gandhi's people disturb the faraway elaphure.
It's the time when humankind's glory and evil come face to face.
It's the time when it's hardest to believe the other side or doubt one's enemies.
It's the time when language gives people hope yet provokes hatred.

It's the time when half the people are perplexed and the other half are worried.
It's the time when the breath of blue whales stirs peace.
It's the time when the stars send off the dead on behalf of relatives.
It's the time when a thousand priests curse a shadow.
It's the time when the faces of strangers start to become distinct.
It's the time when people in the same bed with different dreams now dream of each other.
It's the time when people seemingly together but actually divergent start a cold war.
It's the time when the old is on the verge of collapse and the new hasn't yet arrived.
It's the time when the divine branches declare misfortune or disaster will be averted.
It's the time when black stones conceal white meanings.
It's the time when the sheep of all gods are waiting for Moses to cross the Red Sea.
It's the time when the bull-horn blown by warriors tears you up with grief.
It's the time when the eagle goblet is grasped once again by the poet prophet.
It's the time when the people and living things on the Tower of Babel earnestly engage in peace talks.

Translated by Hu Wei

The Sun Will Still Rise Tomorrow
—*Speech for the Opening Ceremony of the Thirtieth Medellin International Poetry Festival*

My Dear Poet Friends:

In these unusual times, we're coming together to convene the Thirtieth Medellin International Poetry Festival. This is a grand undertaking deserving congratulations from poets and lovers of poetry from all over the world, because we all know that in this moment, a virus that's devastated the entire world, and that's still spreading, has already changed the world as a whole. The virus is the shared enemy of all humankind. People living in different regions of the world have vividly experienced this immense change. In some sense, the shock and impact of this change is no less than that of the two world wars during the previous century.

In reality, this pandemic has already profoundly reconstructed relations between nations, geopolitical relations, relations between different ethnic communities, and between systems with different values, as well as different economic systems. I think this world after the contest between globalization and anti-globalization will enter a second kind of global era that's completely different from the present one. It's precisely in the most difficult times like these that poets and poetry should undertake the majestic mission of leading humanity's spirit. We need to consider defending freedom, fairness, and justice as our shared responsibility. We must speak out in strong voices of protest against all sorts of exclusionism, including fascism, racism, and different forms of terrorism to promote the peace, progress and development of all humankind. We must use poetry to smash barriers and separation in all forms; we must do our part to construct an even more equitable, fair, humane world. And it's precisely because of this that the outstanding Thirtieth Medellin International Poetry Festival is opening here. In closing, please allow me to quote from my long poem, *Split-Open Planet*.

This is an enormous shift, it's longer than a century, it can only be calculated in terms of a millennium.
We can't return to the past, because the old houses have all disappeared.
We can't choose to close ourselves off; no matter what material becomes a high wall, it only implies separation.
We can't choose to resist; as soon as prejudice turns to hate, you or I could die.
We don't need to ask those ancient rivers; their sources are full of prehistory's silence.
Perhaps this was the original enlightenment, diverse civilizations in harmony were all her children.
Give up the difference of three and try hard to find consensus among seven; this isn't putting the problem off on others.
Within a square might be a round possibility; it's not being prejudiced by first impressions.
Let everyone abandon the laws of the forest; this should be better, not viewing oneself as most important.
Let people try to make bright times last longer rather than bestowing darkness on each other.
None of this is a simple method; it's making all participants aware
the future of this planet doesn't just belong to you and me, it belongs to all lives.
I don't know what will happen tomorrow; it's said poets have the ability to foretell the future,
but I won't predict the future, since the boundless oceans didn't leave any traces in the sky.
The light I've praised countless times is now on a triumphant march.
I don't know what will happen tomorrow, but I know the world will be changed.

Yes! No matter what happens, I firmly and steadfastly believe
the sun will still rise tomorrow, dawn's light will be as before, like a lover's eyes.
The warm wind will still blow over the earth's abdomen, mothers and children will still be playing there.
The blue of the sea will still rise with dreams and, at midnight, become the lovenest of stars.
Most people agree labor and creation will still be the main means through which people attain fulfillment.
People will keep living, good and evil will keep accompanying them; the struggle between humankind and itself won't cease.
The entrance to time doesn't have an obvious marker.
Humankind, you must be courageously and exponentially careful.

I wish Medellin International Poetry Festival complete success.
Long live poetry! Long live peace!

Translated by Jami Proctor Xu

Paying Tribute to the Rivers, Mountains, and Oceans
—Acceptance speech for the 2020 Guayaquil International Poetry Award

This is without question a very difficult time for the world, with a terrible disease continuing to spread through many countries. Anyone living on earth right now is faced with this predicament, along with the uncertainty of what will come tomorrow and the anxiety and pain that entails. This is not a pleasant topic. It weighs heavily upon the mind, yet we all must face the reality. From the day's news, we will quickly learn that the numbers of those infected and dying are still rising. To my understanding, this is not a kind of world war in the traditional sense; but in many ways it has fundamentally altered our way of life and how the world functions. These changes have not been piecemeal, but instead have completely shaken the basic relationships between countries, regional politics, and different economic systems. The old rules are losing their efficacy, and new rules have yet to be established or gain public consensus. Whether or not one is willing to accept or acknowledge this situation, the present circumstances undeniably present a dangerous trial in the history of humankind. I do not mean to sensationalize the situation, but the final outcome of this trial will have a direct effect on the fate of the human world, and will fundamentally influence our future and the direction of our development. Although human history has never progressed smoothly and has involved constant struggle and all conceivable misfortunes that dog us like shadows, what is most worrisome is that during a time when we are facing terrible difficulties, in a time when despair and hope coexist, in some parts of the world xenophobia, fascism, racism, terrorism, and other antisocial and irrational beliefs and behaviors have appeared. For their own benefit, some political interest groups have worked endlessly to use a nation's power to manipulate politics and to fabricate ridiculous lies in order to provoke hatred and opposition between peoples. Of course, at the same time, in different parts of the world, we can see thousands of people working to maintain and uphold the principles of unity, justice, peace and cooperation. They guard and honor the U.N. Charter and international law, and protect the environment and ecology we all depend upon for survival. They devote themselves to relieving poverty and defending basic human rights, consider it a sacred responsibility to promote peace and oppose war and further encourage communication and dialogue between different cultures. Perhaps only when we clearly see our common aspirations will we be able to have faith and confidence in the future of humankind.

In short, I am inclined to think that for many people of different nationalities and ethnic identities, it is a heartfelt goal to break through obstacles and barriers, traverse oceans and continents, and offer tribute to others. Accordingly, I would like to sincerely thank Ecuador, this equatorial country across the world from my own. I would also like to thank one secret source of poetic inspiration for me, namely Latin America, which has given birth to many great poets. I am deeply honored to be the recipient of this year's precious award, and to join the list of such illustrious poets as Juan Gelman, Charles Simic, and Jack Hirschman. Thank you. As a poet, I can find no better way to express my deep thanks than to pay tribute to Ecuador, and hope you all will accept my highest respects.

In paying tribute, I mean to include more than just one rich aspect of your country; I offer tribute to your organic multiplicities, to both the singleness and the complexities of your psyche. Indeed, most astounding is that among the thousands of multiplicities, a singularity can be found. I hope that your gardens burst with colorful balloons, candy, the aged and the young, and gunshots are never heard again.

I pay tribute to you not only because of your vast ocean, magnificent mountains, and fertile land, but also because on the tallest peak of Mt. Chimborazo, all the world's existing tribes today can warm themselves with the eternal fire of the Mayan sun and the fission of gold and boulders in the fourth dimension. I hope that all this does not belong merely to the present, but more importantly, still belongs to the distant future as well.

I pay tribute to you not only because you have the magnificent Amazon River, but also because the river has become a symbol of your people's resistance to violence, from antiquity to the present. It makes vanished time like a wild South American cougar, roaring a red roar from its throat, and makes freedom and justice as timely as the morning sun of your future days. I hope that in the depths of your spirit, the reverence for freedom and justice never changes.

I pay tribute to you not only because you can use Spanish to announce to the world your country's famous saying—*Dios, patria y libertad* (God, homeland, and freedom)—but also because in the Quechua-speaking areas, you can use the kernel of a word to enter into a spiritual realm, reawakening the sleeping stars and long-extinct birds. I hope that this ancient language exists even longer than this earth.

I pay tribute to you not only because in your skies condors unceasingly protect the bodies of mothers, making the dawn over the Galápagos Islands glimmer like the eyes of lovers. I pay tribute because, more importantly, you still have poetry that is even more deeply felt than life and death, and you have the moving and compassionate artworks of Oswaldo Guayasamín, who stood on the side of the poor and his Native American brethren throughout his life. I hope that his compassion and love will live on a thousandfold, though indeed I know that the man himself has never really left us.

Ecuador, I wish you all that is newer than history, more distant than reality, and closer than the future. May your people's hands grasp hold of hope and the days of tomorrow. Thank you!

Translated by Eleanor Goodman

A Sheep, a Farmer and a Poet's Steady Gaze

—Presentation of the 2020 "1573 International Poetry Prize" and Preface of Lucina Schynning in Silence of the Nicht: A Selection of Poems by Eiléan Ní Chuilleanáin

I first heard of Eiléan Ní Chuilleanáin through the Irish poet Patrick Cotter. This is not to say that in this age of globalization, Ní Chuilleanáin can be called a global superstar. It is rather the reverse: in a time of internet sensations, poets hold the loneliest place in the crowd. But perhaps it is this stubborn persistence itself that allows the greatness and importance of poets to transcend conventions and the commonplace. There is no doubt that Eiléan Ní Chuilleanáin is a true poet. Her work is deeply rooted in the grand tradition of Irish poetry, and she brings this tradition into a contemporary linguistic context with incomparable creativity. This is not a straightforward continuation, but rather a continuous spiritual reconstruction of an individual's life experience and of an ancient land. Each poem is a life event, and leaves marks of the individual self on eternal time and space. Her poems bear no relationship to popular sentimental works, but instead are like the stones on the bottom of a riverbed. Or one might say they are like newly dug potatoes, unconcerned with complicated rhetorical flourishes, and instead tightly fusing together exacting language and precise shapes. In her work, metaphors and symbols combine into an appropriate and organic whole. Such impeccable purity and simplicity arrives at the essence of life and nature, and is further proof of poetry's enduring value and irreplaceability. Moreover, we believe absolutely that for the Irish—who have historically held animist beliefs that some maintain despite the fact that polytheism has in many cases evolved into monotheistic religions—the existence of William Butler Yeats, whether viewed from a historical or a contemporary angle, was not simply an isolated incident of significance only to the modern Irish poetry scene. The subsequent generations of Irish poets whom the world has embraced demonstrate that he was much more, from his compatriot Seamus Heaney to the others who have carried his torch into the present day, including the outstanding poet Eiléan Ní Chuilleanáin herself. It is not on mere whim that we cross the wide continents and vast oceans to seek out contemporary Irish poetry. The exchange of true poetry does not exist on a single plane; in fact, this exchange does not always happen as part of a collective effort, but is often achieved through the acts of individuals. The dialogues and lines of communication we have developed are more like hidden passageways between souls, and we rejoice at the good fortune of finding the golden key to those passageways in Ireland. This brings to bear the deeply philosophical Chinese expression, "All that is held in the mind will later come to fruition in life." I would like to express my elation at this inevitable meeting between Chinese poets and poetry and the Irish poet Eiléan Ní Chuilleanáin. As I have said, such meetings are far from isolated incidents, since they will inexorably occur over the passage of time, though perhaps we can still consider it one of life's wonders.

Eiléan Ní Chuilleanáin is first and foremost an Irish poet, but at the same time, she is of course a citizen of the world as well. In terms of cultural identity and language, the Gaelic poetic tradition indisputably forms the primary foundation for her poetry. It is self-evident that her poetry also has a special connection to the English language. Here I would like to avoid making a kind of value judgment based on a simplistic idea of a transitional relationship, but I can be certain that those poets who drift between two languages open up previously unimaginable possibilities. Reading Ní Chuilleanáin's work makes me feel as though I am listening to a performance of "uilleann pipes". Even when her poetry is translated from English into a Chinese linguist context, I am still able to perceive echoes of her native tongue, which have mysteriously traversed all boundaries to arrive at my ears. I have thought of translation in a certain sense as a bridge, but even in switching from one bridge to another, something immutable remains, namely some ineffable, inherent, mysterious essence. Roman Jakobson, a founding member of the Prague School of linguistics, was of the opinion that patterns from the internal structure of language and the earliest original language are, like human genes, always faintly perceptible in the background, and their existence is fixed and unchanging. More than a brilliant Gaelic poet, Eiléan Ní Chuilleanáin is also a highly significant poet in multilingual writing circles. The translation of her work into many different languages demonstrates the value and uniqueness of her voice. This particular value and uniqueness implies a more fundamental and broad significance, and it is for this reason that her work can cross continents and oceans to be lauded by people of diverse ethnicities and backgrounds.

The poetic world she creates is vast and far-reaching, set against the backdrop of an ancient yet youthful Ireland. Her work offers us a new interpretation of ancient myths and fairy tales, while at the same time revealing the deepest spiritual experiences people can have in the midst of ordinary life. Her quiet, austere, and highly tactile poetry leads us to the highest respect and admiration, and to the conviction that she is a successor to a great poetic tradition and an expert practitioner who can teach us the ancient language of the imagination. Therefore, we are delighted to present the 2020 "1573 International Poetry Prize" to the outstanding contemporary Irish poet Eiléan Ní Chuilleanáin.

Translated by Eleanor Goodman

Eiléan Ní Chuilleanáin born in 1942, an Irish poet and translator. She is the laureate of the 2020 "1573 International Poetry Prize" of China.

Let Poetry be the Path Leading to Each Heart: Answers to the Questions from the Organizing Committee of 14th World Poetry Festival of Venezuela

Freddy Ñañez: I've noticed that your poetry has a double influence:

-A) on one hand is its constant approach to the voice of a Lorca, Whitman, Neruda and Vallejo, Yevtushenko, Mayakovsky to name a few, where your poetry merges in the temporalities and aesthetics of a poetic universalization.

Jidi Majia: Yes. My poetry is under the influences of various aspects. One of them is the classic Chinese poetry, including the classical Romantic poets represented by Qu Yuan, the follow-up Tang poetry and Song lyrics as well as modern Chinese poetry. All of them from different perspectives have me inherit the poetry tradition in Chinese language lasting for thousands of years. In addition, I also obtain rich nourishment from the epics and lyrics of the Yi people. The lyricism in my poetry mostly comes from these poems full of folk charm with ballad characteristics. Of course, the influence from foreign poetry in my writing career is self-evident. In many places I stated that besides the influences of poetry in Europe, North America and Russia, undoubtedly the poetry of Latin America is one of the important sources affecting my poem writing. If we call the group of poets a republic, Lorca, Whitman, Neruda and Vallejo are elders and elder brothers in a big family belonging to me. Yet Yevtushenko and Mayakovsky are poets whose poetic nature is more similar to mine. I have a sort of natural friendliness with them. Just like the animals who always search for their own kind through the scent, I find a lot of similarities from them, especially how poets establish stronger ties between their own poems and the people and eras. Certainly, they have set shinning examples for me. While facing the masses, heir works are not isolated but always glowing with enthusiasm to the era and life. It is they who taught me that real poetry with genuine affinity to the people strikes a responsive chord in the hearts of the majority.

Freddy Ñañez: -B) on the other hand, your marked identity ancestry that leads you to travel in your own region and identify culture: the Yi cosmogony.

Let's talk about that experience from the local to the universal and of being universal without sacrificing local identity.

JIdi Majia: In this world there is no abstract "poet", just like there is no abstract "human". The poets do not lose their cultural identities and social roles due to their poetry having universal significance. On the contrary, the cultural identities and social roles of poets have never changed since the very beginning. This fact is especially applicable to those national poets in the true sense of the word. With distinct individual colors and life experiences, their works can genuinely sublimate through local experience to present universalization. Such examples in world history of literature are too many to recount. The prominent Russian poet Pushkin, the Polish poet Adam Mickiewicz, the German poet Goethe and the Italian poet Dante are all models in this aspect. Their works belong to not only their own nations but also the whole world. Pushkin is the first poet having a decisive influence on me in my childhood. He is the very reason that I am determined to be a poet of nation.

Freddy Ñañez: There is a recurring theme in your poetry: the Homeland. This has a very different meaning in China from what is understood by the homeland in the West. Can you tell us about the millennial anguish of your people for the unity of the country?

Jidi Majia: China is a multi-ethnic country. Though in the history it experienced a very complicated process of ethnic integration, the most important part is all ethnic groups in China have preserved their own cultural traditions and histories while China becomes a pluralistic community and a big family of nationalities, which is greatly different from many other countries. Majority of the ethnic groups living throughout the land of China are genuine aboriginal inhabitants; the areas they immigrate to and live in have countless ties for thousands of years with this land on which they were born and brought up. I think the homeland I extol in my poems is not only a geographic concept; more importantly, it is also a spiritual and cultural symbol. As a poet, I started to travel between two languages since childhood. Luckily, I have been nourished motherly by ancient Chinese and similarly ancient Yi language. Frankly speaking, I obtain magical imagination and endless inspiration mainly from these two ancient languages.

Freddy Ñañez: Your book From Snow Leopard to Mayakovsky is a compilation of poems. Was this selection made with Spanish readers in mind? What were the criteria?

Jidi Majia: Sorry, but this selection of poems is not made particularly for Spanish readers. It has been earlier translated into different languages and printed in many countries. Its English translation was published in San Francisco. Yet it is especially my pleasure that this book has been published in many countries of Latin America. This is surely my honor, for I always regard Latin America another source of my poetry. My love for this magical land seems inherent. I have been to a majority of Latin American countries, and when I saw local inhabitants over there, I felt as if I were back to my hometown, the Grand Liangshan Mountain inhabited by Yi ethnic group in compact communities in Sichuan Province. We can say that the love for Latin America is an instinct of mine. It seems that all of these have mystical links with something private in my blood and my soul. Instead of calling it predetermination, I prefer to regard it as a certain original, primitive memory that I can find on this soil.

Freddy Ñañez: When we talk about Chinese poetry we always think of the Tang. And that is why everyone expects from poetry written in China a kind of restraint and mystical and measured temperament or romanticism and melancholy. How is Chinese poetry today?

Jidi Majia: As you said, Chinese poetry has a long history of development. We can say that Chinese poetry, with its uniqueness, is more eligible to represent the distinguishing characteristic of oriental poetry. Tang Dynasty is a golden age of not only Chinese poetry but also world poetry, for in that historical period there is no other country which the emergence of such a large number of poetic geniuses is concentrated. The classical Chinese poetry does not deeply influence the writing of poets of later ages but also have an important influence on the late Western symbolism poetry in the end of 19th Century and early 20th Century. By translating Tang poems and Japanese haiku, the American poet Ezra Pound established the spiritual and formable reconstructions between Western poetry and Eastern poetry. It seems that contemporary Chinese poetry is more diversified. The vertical inheritance and horizontal adaptation allows Chinese poetry in our eyes to have various art characteristics. Or, maybe it is such variety that fills the future of Chinese poetry with unlimited possibilities. Personally, I think now is one of the best times of prosperity and development of Chinese poetry.

Freddy Ñañez: Your poetry has a metaphorical charge that makes it very rich in mythical images and gives it a frenetic rhythm similar to the oral narration of ancient peoples. Is this your way of honoring the roots of your Yi people?

Jidi Majia: There is no need for reticence that metaphor is common in my poems. Besides the reason that my poetry needs such metaphor, it is more important that in my poetry there is a lot similar to divinity. This is not my groundless creation; it is the animistic consciousness of my ethnic group that makes my poems seem like endowment from the deities. Even in today's experiencing modernization, the Yi people in my hometown are still traveling between the real world and the realm of spirits in the depth of their consciousness. In this regard, the Mexican writer Juan Rulfo's Pedro Páramo is extremely similar with the mountain life of we Yi people. As an ancient ethnic group, we currently go through a process of modernization just like the majority of aboriginal nationalities of this world do. Spiritually and mentally we always expect to go back to where we started. However, it seems that our genuine return to that origin is nothing but expectation and longing. We want to go back just because we cannot. Many of my poems express such feeling, which is like what Martinican poet Aimé Césaire expressed in his famous poem Return to My Native Land. Actually, this is a world theme for modern people.

Freddy Ñañez: You were deputy governor of the Qinghai Province, and now you are a member of Standing Committee of the National People's Congress. You are therefore a man of poetry and politics. How do you manage to combine these two seemingly different worlds?

Jidi Majia: Not all politicians are able to be good poets. Similarly, not all poets can show outstanding capabilities in the political realm. As a matter of fact, there have been already lots of vivid examples in this aspect. In the world there are always someone who can combine these two seemingly different worlds; there's no lack of such people among poets and politicians. Just now I mentioned Martinican poet Aimé Césaire, who is a prominent politician and a poetic genius at the same time. Léopold Senghor, studying in Paris together with Aimé Césaire when they were young, is another famous figure with dual role as statesman and poet. He is the first president of Senegal after its independence. As a poet, he absolutely holds a vital position in the poetic circles of French language in 20th Century. He is among the few Africans who are selected as "the Immortals" of the French Academy. Of course, there are many such poets. For example, the French poets Paul Éluard and Louis Aragon, and the Chilean poet Pablo Neruda we know very well, are all great poets with the role of political activist. Many journalists have asked me the questions concerned, and I need to explain that by its nature poet is not a profession, but, more accurately, a social role and nothing else. People familiar with ancient history of China must know that the majority of ancient Chinese poets have taken up posts of different ranks. The typical examples include Wang Wei of Tang Dynasty and Su Dongpo of Song Dynasty.

Freddy Ñañez: Venezuela and China are two countries that have strengthened their ties of friendship. Do you have any expectations for this to go beyond trade and government cooperation and become a cultural alliance?

Jidi Majia: There is no doubt that China and Venezuela are two countries of brotherhood, that we have strong ties in many aspects. In my opinion, besides more to do in trade and government cooperation, indeed we need to enhance the in-depth communication and link of culture. In international communication, we will persevere in multilateralism and oppose unilateralism; particularly, we will not turn a blind eye to the similar hegemony and bullying conducts of certain countries. In this aspect, we are glad to seed that our two governments and two peoples have spoken with one voice in combating imperialism, neo-fascism, terrorism and all trends of exclusivism. Yet it is necessary for us to carry out wider exchange and dialogues in the cultural area and to walk into each other's heart through more diversified ways and channels, so that we can form a genuine cultural alliance. I believe this is not only a good wish of we poets but also an expectation of our two peoples, and I think through our common, relentless efforts, we will definitely realize all these wishes. I expect to visit your beautiful country after the end of global pandemic.

Freddy Ñañez: We would like to finish for you to read us a couple of poems from this book.

Jidi Majia: OK. This is my honor and something I am willing to do. So I will recite a poem dedicating to Spanish poet Lorca. It is entitled as Looking For Federico García Lorca.

In Search of Federico García Lorca

I go seeking you—
Federico García Lorca
Beneath Granada's open skies
Your shadow pervades each draught of air
I pass along the avenues where you strolled
Your name brings no echo
Only watery gleams from Guadalquivir River
Waver in the tops of orange and olive trees;
In Granada, I devotedly pay visits
To every house you resided in
From the cradle you slept in as a baby
(Though its songs and rocking have stopped)
To the desk where you wrote heartrending ballads.
Federico García Lorca—
I go seeking you, not just to seek the Andalusia
Where flags were set tossing and twirling

By your life and gigantic death
And guitars go on weeping today
But because your soul and graceful manner
And the unseen sadness beneath your joy
Have covered this green land in silvery light
Federico García Lorca—
A true clairvoyant of poetry, not just for the sake
Of becoming a poet did he come into this world
Yet only through mediumship of language and sound
Could he become a true poet chieftain
Federico García Lorca—
Although your keen feeling for written words gave you
A light like ability to extract the forms of things
With your God-given words you would never be
An artisan who drowned words in ornate displays;
Your poems are lips of the open sky,
They are eagerness of springwater, cranium of dusk
They are stars in braided birdsong, thoughts in seclusion
They are wheat ears known to crickets, pastoral cup
They are tiny bells of laurel, mist obscured moonlight
They are a chilly aureole, foxfire on snowy ground
Heart that stabs the sharp sword, sleep of a skeleton
Gall on the tongue tip, tambourine at death's door
They are a throat on fire, a vein cut open
The front of death, the sad wind of redness
They are stubborn blood, skillfulness at dying
Federico García Lorca—
At last we really made it to Andalusia
Only now do we know why your poetry holds
The taste of living blood, the gumption of metal!

Translated by Hu Wei

A Round of Applause for a World that is Diverse, Rich, Always Different and Symbiotic
—*Address to the 14th Venezuelan World Poetry Festival*

Dear Friends and Fellow Poets,

Needless to say, humanity is at an extremely difficult moment today, and the epidemic that has ravaged the world is still spreading and is still very serious in some countries and places, and there is no doubt that this is a common human catastrophe that we are worried about every day because it has not yet been eradicated, all the more so because it comes at a time when there are political and interest groups that do not respect putting human life first, there is still endless political manipulation and attempts to stir up confrontation and hatred among human beings, which, of course, are despised and firmly condemned by the majority of peace-loving people in this world. Some say that humanity has today entered a post-epidemic era, others say that it would be more accurate to define it as the era of sub-globalization, because this epidemic has fundamentally changed our reality and our lives, and while we cannot set aside these more concrete and distressing realities, we cannot afford to lose the hope and the courage to move forward into tomorrow at such a time, and because of this. The fact that we have come together to participate in the fourteenth Venezuelan World Poetry Festival, which has special significance, is yet another proof of the importance of communication and dialogue and of the inadvisability of unilateralism, both in international politics and in people-to-people exchanges, while multilateralism has always been a fundamental principle shared by the majority of countries, and the breaking down of all obstacles and barriers has made the world a better place to live in. It is the common will of all freedom-loving and justice-seeking peoples who advocate peace and oppose war, because the foundation and core of this universal and commonly perceived choice derives from our identification with a world that is plural, rich, always different and symbiotic. Biological diversity has proven its undeniable importance, and the disruption of the biological chain of this planet at any point, even the disappearance of some of the so-called weakest organisms in the least noticed, can cause unexpected damage to our overall life cycle system, and when this damage is not stopped by us, the ultimate consequences are often catastrophic. Quantum theory is one of the two cornerstones of modern physics, which reveals the basic laws of the microscopic material world, and more importantly, it tells us about the infinite separability of particles and the mysterious relationships between related particles. It is not metaphysical metaphysics that the pain of an inseparable part of the cosmic world, perhaps just at its most minute end, also reaches out to some more distant being with a connection to this, I think. The diversity of cultures and the different ways of life of the world's peoples require today's human beings to defend, both practically and morally, this sacred and inviolable right, and if this right is elevated to different nation-states, then it is equally the right of the people of that country to choose the social system and the way of development, and no external force should interfere with it. That is why, in full accordance with the principles established by international law and the humanitarian imperative, we firmly oppose and reject the blockade and embargo against any sovereign state with a legitimate government, and we, as poets, will unreservedly stand with the Venezuelan people, with Venezuelan poets who love their country and who love humanity as a whole, and I am convinced that, with the joint efforts of all, the Fourteenth Venezuelan World Poetry Festival will be a resounding success, and allow me to conclude with a fragment of my long poem, "Split-Open Planet":

Is this the planet creating us
or are we changing the planet?

When the split-open planet spins the wheel on volition's forehead,
all lives will run under the ever-unchanging sun.
The masks on the gods of creation will glimmer in the boundless dome of the heavens.
That omnipresent light will return from the sky's womb into the dark, pure air of another space, like the liquid womb.
That's our planet's, the only blue,
a virgin olive floating beyond the imagination.
That's our planet, a single water droplet that doesn't fall,
the metaphysical gemstone that can't be casually named.
It's a flame not extinguished by life or death, transformed by the creator.
We don't need to be mediums, even up to the present,
we can find its genes in the earth, oceans, forests and rivers.
That's our planet, it nurtures all lives.
In spite of wars, plagues, disasters or regime changes,
it's never ceased to nourish and be charitable towards life.
When we caress its body, even though it's beautiful as before, we can see scars on it that break our hearts.
This is our planet, no matter who you are, what race you belong to,
no matter which place on its body you're living in,
we should all gather together for its vitality and beauty.
Saving the planet can never be separated from saving ourselves.
O, goddess Pumolieyi,[1] please let me borrow your needle that sews skulls,
and that ball of white-wool yarn in your hands, because I want to sew together this planet we've already split open.

Translated by Fu Hao

---

1 Pumolieyi, a goddess in the Nuosu creation myths, the virgin mother of the hero Zhyga Alu.

Weeping for Der Zor

— A Preface to Sona Van's A LIBRETTO FOR THE DESERT and the Laudation for 573 International Poetry Prize of 2019

Weeping for Der Zor, weeping for bones under the desert of Der Zor, weeping for wind, weeping for the dawn of darkness, weeping for the twilight blinking in the universe. Tell me, who is weeping? Because the weeping is still crying and never stops! Weeping for the breasts, weeping for the wombs, weeping for the babies alive and dead, weeping for the send-off without reunion, weeping for the desperate silence of women. Tell me, who is weeping? Because the weeping is still crying and never stops! Weeping for oblivion, weeping for the fading evil, weeping for elaborated lies, weeping for the misfortune of humankind, weeping for all lives. Tell me, who is weeping? Because the weeping is still crying and never stops! This person weeping by poetry, this witness, is Sona Van, a loyal daughter of Armenia.

For Sona Van, Der Zor desert is a symbol, a metaphor, a wound passing through time. That is why this eminent poet presents to this world and us a part of Armenian national history, which is too sad to reflect, by pure poetry. Reading these dolorous verses, we dive into somewhere deeper and quieter through the entrance of each word, experiencing the pain of life unconsciously. When we feel such a pain vividly, for a brief instant we will find it transcends the individual life experience to become a part of common perception in the spirits and emotions of humanity. Leaving aside the contribution of these poems in the sense of text, we people living for today are already shocked terribly enough just by the philosophic thoughts about life and death as well as the question and inquiry regarding the darkest part of humanity in these poetic lines. In front of such poetry, those poems without soul and texture of life will never be considered as real poetry. A poet like Sona Van is the very reason why we are full of confidence about poetry and, of course, filled with expectation for the glorious future of human beings.

Translated by Hai An

Biographies of translators

Denis Mair holds an M. A. in Chinese from Ohio State University and has taught at University of Pennsylvania. He translated autobiographies by the philosopher Feng Youlan (Hawaii University Press) and the Buddhist monk Shih Chen hua (SUNY Press). His translation of art criticism by Zhu Zhu was published by Hunan Fine Arts Press (2009). He's translated poetry by Jidi Majia, Yan Li, Mai Cheng, Meng Lang, and many others.

Eleanor Goodman (Gu Ailing) is a Research Associate at the Harvard Fairbank Center. Her book of translations, *Something Crosses My Mind: Selected Poems of Wang Xiaoni* (Zephyr Press, 2014) was the recipient of a 2013 PEN/Heim Translation Grant and winner of the 2015 Lucien Stryk Prize. The book was also shortlisted for the International Griffin Prize in 2015. A collection of her own poetry, *Nine Dragon Island,* was shortlisted for the Drunken Boat First Book Prize.

Jami Proctor Xu is a poet, translator, artist. She writes in Chinese and English. She grew up in Tucson, Arizona, and currently splits her time between Northern California and China. Her Chinese poetry collections include *Shimmers* (EMS: Du Shi Series, 2013) and *Suddenly Starting to Dance* (Yi Press, 2016). Her English chapbook, *Hummingbird Ignites a Star,* was published in 2014. Her poems appear frequently in journals and anthologies in China and the U.S. Jami has translated collections by the Chinese poets Jidi Majia and Song Lin. In 2013 she received a Zhujiang Poetry Award for a non-Chinese poet who has made a contribution to contemporary Chinese poetry.

Huang Shaozheng, who translated Jidi Majia's literary and cultural speeches of this volume, is an independent translation scholar and translator based in Qinghai Normal University with two monographs and five translations to his credit. Major works include *Translation Or Creation?* (2004), *Translation Paid In Gold* (2012), *Prophet* by Gibran-A new Translation (2012), *In the Name of Land and Life-Jidi Majia's Literary and Cultural Speeches* (2013), New Testament (2015).

Fu Hao lives and works as research professor of English in Beijing. He writes poetry in Chinese and English and translates from English, Sanskrit, Greek, Latin, French and Japanese. He has won various literary awards, including the Liang Shih-ch'iu Literary Prize for Poetry Translation from Taiwan and published two books of poetry, three collections of essays, one booklet on T'ai Chi Ch'uan, two monographs of literary criticism and over thirty volumes of translation of world literature, including *The Complete Lyrical Poems of W. B. Yeats, Amorushatakam, Collected Poems of John Donne,* and *Selected Poems of William Carlos Williams.*

Hu Wei, born in 1981 in Beijing, is a translator of poetry. Graduated with a Major in English from Beijing Language and Culture University, he now serves as a staff member of International Liaison Department of the China Writers Association. He has translated the English version of *A Libretto for the Desert*, a poetry selection of Armenian poet Sona Van, and poem selection *Lucina Schynning in Silence of the Nicht* by Irish poet Eiléan Ní Chuilleanáin, into Chinese. His translation of poems and essays of poets from Greece, Israel, Spain, U.S., Austria, etc. were published in journals such as The Yangtze River Poetry Journal, Writer and Stars.

Hai An, ***pseudonym for Dingjun LI,*** Chinese scholar-poet and translator in China-Australia Creative Writing Centre, Fudan University, born in 1965, now resides in Shanghai, China. He has published over ten books of poetry as the author, translator and editor, including *Selected Poems of Hai An* (Beijing, 2001), *Elegy* (Long Poem, Taiwan, 2012). As the winner of the STA-2016 Translation Achievement Award issued by the Shanghai Translator Association, he was invited to attend several international poetry festivals including the 48th International Poetry Evenings in Struga, Macedonia (2009) and China-Australia Creative Writing Workshops at Fudan and Curtin University (2016-2019).

www.ingramcontent.com/pod-product-compliance
Lightning Source LLC
Chambersburg PA
CBHW030516080526
44586CB00011B/210